MR RUGBY LEIGH

MR RUGBY LEIGH

The Tommy Sale Story

Written with Andy Hampson

Scratching Shed Publishing Ltd

First published by Scratching Shed Publishing Ltd in 2010
Registered in England & Wales No. 6588772.
Registered office:
47 Street Lane, Leeds, West Yorkshire. LS8 1AP

www.scratchingshedpublishing.co.uk

ISBN 978-0956252616

Unless stated otherwise, all photographs are from the personal collection of Tommy Sale

Cover photograph: Tommy Sale dives over for his second try in Widnes' 1950 Challenge Cup semi-final win over Bradford.

Back cover photograph: Tommy Sale welcomes new head coach Ian Millward back to Leigh (Maurice Jones).

A catalogue record for this book is available from the British Library.

Typeset in Warnock Pro Semi Bold and Palatino

Printed and bound in the United Kingdom by
L.P.P.S.Ltd, Wellingborough, Northants, NN8 3PJ

In memory of my much-missed wife Evelyne,
whom I neglected too often by putting rugby first
and family second.

Acknowledgements

I cannot thank Tommy Sale enough for making *Mr Rugby Leigh* such an enjoyable project to work on throughout 2009. I am privileged to have been able to help him write his incredible life story and I hope I have been able to do it justice. Tommy has been wonderful company and become a good friend. I hope to see him at plenty more Leigh matches in the future.

I would also like to thank the following for their assistance at various stages in the production of this book: Matt Sale, Ronnie Sale, Jean Mangnall, Mike Latham, Dave Jones, Julie McKiernan, Mark Taylor, Emma Stoney, Frank Yates, Stephen Yates, Ray Fletcher, Andrew Parkinson, Dave Parkinson, Ian Townsend, Debbie Townsend, Maurice Jones, Bob Shuttleworth, Chris Lines, Mike Appleton, Danny Doherty, Sarah Smith, Pat Cluskey, Bill Hampson, Pam Hampson, Sheila Swift, Bernard Swift.

I must also express my gratitude to Colin Hutton, Alex Murphy, Mick Martyn, Dave Chisnall, John Woods, Keith Latham, Paul Rowley, Ian Millward, Arthur Thomas, Allan Rowley and Lord Peter Smith for their heartfelt tributes; and the Rt Hon Andy Burnham, Member of Parliament for Leigh, for his foreword.

Thanks also to Tony Hannan and Phil Caplan at Scratching Shed for showing interest in publishing Tommy's story.

Finally, I cannot end without thanking my wife Rachel for her patience and understanding whilst working on something which at times must have seemed like an obsession.

Andy Hampson, 2010

Andy Hampson is a sports journalist for the Press Association.

Contents

Contents (*continued*)

*

Foreword

The Rt Hon Andy Burnham
Member of Parliament for Leigh

You will struggle to find a more popular man in Leigh than Tommy Sale. Tommy has devoted his life to the town and its people and remains as committed as ever in his 90s.

Tommy is the friendly face and president of Leigh Rugby League Football Club, to whom he has given more than 80 years of almost unbroken service. He started as a scoreboard operator at the age of 10, grew up to play for and captain the club and then went on to fill a number of administrative roles. He now keeps himself busy as the team's timekeeper and statistician and seldom misses a game, home or away.

Tommy has been with the club through the good times and the bad times and his dedication has known no bounds. He was a key figure in the building of the old Hilton Park ground after the War, working around the clock to ensure the club had a place of their own to play. That ground served the club for more than six decades until the recent move to the new Leigh Sports Village.

Mr Rugby Leigh

Yet it is not only for rugby that Tommy is renowned. He was a highly respected teacher and headmaster at St Peter's primary school for many years and took on many other jobs within the community. He served on the old Leigh Borough Council, was on the St Peter's Church Council and has undertaken many fundraising activities for local clubs and societies. He has also coached a lot of junior rugby teams, while many people might know him as the former owner of a town centre sweet shop. It is not surprising there are few places in Leigh he can visit without being recognised.

Tommy greets everyone with a smile and is always pleasant and engaging. He has time for everyone and few can leave his company without having been touched by his warmth and gregariousness.

Tommy is rightly regarded as a legend throughout Leigh.

The Rt Hon Andy Burnham
Member of Parliament for Leigh

*

Introduction

People ask me how I have lived so long but the answer is simple; Leigh Rugby League Football Club. The club is my lifeblood and has been since I was a child. Even now, at the age of 91, I still live for the place and am there, in the office, almost every day. It is a life I have thoroughly enjoyed and I have not regretted a single moment. I got my first job at Leigh as a scoreboard operator more than 80 years ago and have served in just about every capacity since; as a player, captain, supporters' club president, director, scout, assistant secretary, timekeeper, statistician and president. Only the coaching role has eluded me, but I was never interested in that.

I saw my doctor recently and she asked me if I had ever smoked. I said I hadn't touched tobacco for more than 50 years and even then I'd only ever puffed on the odd cigar. The doctor immediately suggested that must be the main reason why I have maintained my health into my nineties.

Yet whilst that might have helped, I quickly pointed out that my wife Evelyne used to smoke like a chimney, about 20 a day, and she lived until she was 91. I said what really keeps me going is Leigh rugby club.

After retiring as a headmaster in 1982, I struggled to handle the resulting emptiness. After about two months I said to Evelyne that if I didn't find something else to do quickly I'd be dead in 12 months. I knew I'd simply get depressed. So I went back to the club and have been going there almost every day since to work on a voluntary basis. I don't spend as much time there as I used to but it continues to give me a lot of pleasure. In short, it has given me a life.

I am recognised almost everywhere I go in Leigh and I am always bowled over by the warmth and generosity of the people. I love getting out, meeting and talking to people. It keeps me involved and my brain ticking over. My children ask me: "Dad, can't you go anywhere without people stopping to talk to you?" I say not in Leigh I can't. Every time I go into Leigh I am approached by well-wishers, often people I don't know, and I always enjoy chatting with them. I can usually tell when it's an old pupil because they'll still address me as Mr Sale. Most people call me Tommy, which is great.

I go to Sainsbury's every Saturday morning and not so long ago a little boy came up to me and grabbed my hand. "Are you Tommy Sale?" he asked. I looked down and this little face gazed back. I said I was indeed Tommy Sale and he then told me how nice it was to meet me. I was so touched, it was wonderful.

Things have changed at the club recently with the move from Hilton Park, a ground which I miss dearly. Over the years that stadium became a home from home for me and Evelyne used to claim, only half-jokingly, that I actually lived there, so little did I see of her at times. I was one of the people in charge of building the ground after the Second World War and I had many happy times there as a player, a spectator and working in the office afterwards. The club now have a lovely new home at Leigh Sports Village but it isn't the same. It will never be Hilton Park.

Given my love of Leigh, it may therefore come as a surprise to some that I consider the best years of my playing career to have been at Widnes. I had a couple of seasons there after being told I was surplus to requirements at Hilton Park and it went better than I could possibly have imagined. The undoubted highlight was in 1950 when, just a few months after leaving Leigh, I captained the Chemics in front of more than 94,000 at Wembley in the Challenge Cup final. That was an incredible experience, even though we lost, and one I shall never forget.

That was the closest I came to glory as a player but, as a director, I was able to celebrate going one better 21 years later as Leigh pulled off their magnificent and unexpected Challenge Cup final win over Leeds. It was the greatest moment in the club's history and another amazing memory.

Rugby league has given me so much pleasure and has been a huge part of my life for so long. It is because of the game that I came back to Leigh after serving overseas during the Second World War, when I seriously considered staying on in the Army. Instead, I came home and later found a great new career as a teacher. I worked at the same junior school, St Peter's in Leigh, for 33 years, the last 13 of which were as headmaster. Having come from a humble background, that is an achievement of which I am very proud.

Throughout my life I have had my ups and downs but I believe I have been very lucky and the ups have outnumbered the downs. I was happily married for 66 years and there are plenty of people out there who don't even get 66 years altogether. It does get lonely at times now – family can be a nuisance but you miss them when they are not there – but I have been very fortunate. All I have done is try to enjoy myself and, as I look back over my life in the coming pages, I hope I can share some of that with you.

Tommy Sale, 2010

*

Chapter One

I may be a familiar face in Leigh but my name has not travelled the four miles or so to Hindsford, the small town between Atherton and Tyldesley where it all began for me. I know this because on my 90th birthday I drove back there to visit the house in Robert Street where, in the back bedroom, I was born on July 21, 1918. When I arrived I knocked on the door rather sheepishly and a lady answered. I introduced myself and told her why I was visiting. She had no idea who I was but was very interested in my tale and kindly invited me in for a cup of tea and to have a look around.

The house used to be my grandparents' and as she showed me the different rooms the memories came flooding back. I looked at the coal fire and could remember vividly my grandmother, Nain as I knew her because she was Welsh, sitting in front of it with a mug of Guinness. She would lean forward to stick the poker in the fire and then take it out and dip it in her stout. It added iron, she always said. It seems like a crazy thing to do but Nain Sale lived until she was 98, so perhaps that is the secret of long life, drinking Guinness after crudely adding iron with a hot poker! She and her husband, my grandfather, were very kind to me. Taid, as I knew him, used to take me shooting from time to time with his double-barrelled gun. We'd go all round the fields of Hindsford. Other times he'd offer to take me for days out to Southport, Blackpool or the zoo at Belle Vue. I had many good weekends with my grandparents but it was actually the change of scenery I appreciated most, getting out of my parents' house. Life at home was miserable because of one man – my father. Any time I spent away from him was a blessing.

Charles Henry Sale, my dad, was a nasty, wicked man. He was an alcoholic who squandered his money and beat his wife. My mother, Gertrude Elizabeth Sale, was an angel and quite what she did to deserve a man like him I'll never know. He treated her terribly and made her life a misery. I used to shake like a leaf listening to him shouting at Mum. When he was sober, a nicer chap you couldn't wish to meet, but those times were few and far between. When he was drunk, as he usually was, he was a villain, a really horrid individual. He had no concern for his family whatsoever, only his beer and his own health. I hated him. He rarely needed an excuse to hit me and I look back on most of my childhood with absolute horror.

I gave my dad a good hiding when I was 30 and I only wish I could have done it 30 years earlier. I'd gone home one Sunday after my mother had invited me round for tea, as she did every week. I went in and saw her sat in the corner with a huge black eye. I asked how that had happened and she admitted Dad had done it. I was furious and decided that was the final straw.

I asked where he was and she pointed me towards the kitchen. I was very angry but kept my cool as I walked through to find him. He was sitting there eating at the table and didn't even acknowledge me. I calmly walked over and opened the back door behind him. I then moved back towards him and when I got near I picked his plate up and pushed it into his face. I then dragged him up from the table, pulled him outside and hit him hard. My mother tried to stop me but I said he'd had it coming a long time. What I did was enough to send him to hospital for stitches. He ran out into the street crying, "Look at what my famous son has done to me", but the neighbours knew what he was like and sympathy was in short supply. I laid the law down to him firmly after that. "If you put a finger on my mother again, I won't put you in hospital," I told him. "I'll put you in the cemetery."

He never did touch her again after that, but he still got to her mentally. He'd have been about 50 by the time of that incident and he'd never learned from any of his mistakes over the years. How he could do what he did, I don't know. He wasted our money all the time and there was never any left for food. He always had to have his drink and his infernal Woodbines. They came before feeding the family.

He even thumped his own father without reason once. I think I had justification for hitting my dad, but he had none to strike his. Taid Sale was not like his son. He was very good to me and in many respects did the job my dad should have been doing. He took me out regularly and that is something Dad never did. I also remember well the times he used to go off shooting in north Wales and come back with a few rabbits for us. I used to love eating rabbit. It is almost as nice as chicken and we ate it a lot in those days. But Taid was never the same after being hit by Dad. It made him a sick man and he never recovered. It was so sad.

My dad never showed the slightest bit of interest in my rugby career either. He just couldn't be bothered. He never came to watch me play, not even at Wembley. Most fathers would have been proud to see a son lead a side out in a cup final, but not him. He couldn't even say what position I played. He was a terrible father and I couldn't stand him.

He died in my arms years later and I admit I did not shed a tear. I did not even go to his funeral. I had no intention of seeing him off. That sounds bad but the truth is I was glad to see the back of him. I visited him when he was in Atherleigh home in his final weeks, I kept faith in him in that sense, but I was not upset when he passed away in front of me. I remember it vividly as he had started mumbling and the nurse said she thought he was going. When I got back home afterwards I told Mum he had died and that she would finally be able to enjoy some peace. I was pleased she at least managed to get another six years without him.

Still, some good did come from it all as it taught me one thing: how not to treat your kids. I had four children and none of them could say the same about their dad. Two of them have died now but I loved all four of them to bits and I know they loved me. I made sure I did my duty to them. I tried to give them everything and they always had good holidays. They are wonderful kids and I am very lucky to have had them. They all went on to get good jobs and their children have in turn done well for themselves too. I cherish the time I get to spend with them all. My daughter Jean lives only just around the corner and my son Ronnie is also nearby. Jean calls every night and is always doing little things for me while Ronnie joins me at matches and takes me to the cricket club for a drink every Friday night. My grandsons also call round regularly and I go down to the rugby union club, where they all play and which is just down the road, for the odd tipple too. Mind you, times have changed because that's not a place I have always been welcome. Years ago I was once thrown out of the clubhouse because they suspected, rightly as it happened, that I was scouting for Leigh RL. Thankfully, we can laugh about all that now and I enjoy my visits there these days.

I lived in Hindsford until I was about four years of age when my parents split up. My mum had grown tired of my dad's errant ways and moved out, taking me and my sister Edith with her to live at her sister's in Leigh. I've been living in the town ever since.

My dad was a labourer at Chanters Colliery in Hindsford and he'd often come home and say he'd lost his wages. He'd lost them alright, but only in the sense that he had frittered them away on booze or gambling at dominoes or cards. On paydays, instead of coming home, he'd head straight down to the pub and roll in at about 10 or 11 o'clock absolutely kaylied. I don't know how he thought Mum was supposed to make ends meet without any money. What sort of a husband or father behaves like that?

Things came to a head after he was injured at work and received a large payout in compensation. He got about £2,000, maybe more, which in those days was an extraordinary amount of money. My mother hoped to use some to set up a small business, which could have proved quite a goldmine, but Dad had different ideas. He stashed the money in a tin box on top of the wardrobe and locked it up with a key he always kept on his person. He soon took to taking handfuls of cash from the box, locking it back up and then disappearing for two or three days, sometimes a week. He only used to come back when he wanted some more money. It wore my mother down and that is when she left him.

We moved to my Auntie May's on Norbury Street, off Wigan Road, and stayed there for two or three years. Yet my dad was neither gone nor forgotten. He kept coming back and pestering my mum to get together again and eventually she agreed. I was still only young but this proved a major turning point in my life. As a result of their reconciliation, we moved to a new council house in Cecil Street, close to the Mather Lane Bridge. Now that bridge might only be notable these days as a point where the road crosses the little-used Bridgewater Canal, but back then it was almost adjacent to the home of Leigh Rugby League Football Club. It was through moving there that I first got interested in rugby league and I started following the club avidly.

But apart from the rugby, life in Cecil Street had little else to commend it. Whenever I go past there these days I always call number four the house of horrors. My dad made it hell. With no money for food we were always hungry and many times all I had for my tea was a sugar butty. The clothes I used to wear were just rags and I used to lie in bed shivering at night because all I had for blankets were two old overcoats. We simply couldn't afford anything better. I was also thrown out of the Bedford Church choir once because I was embarrassed about my lack of decent footwear and had not been attending services. I missed two or three Sundays and the vicar told me I had to leave because I was not committed enough. Yet the real reason was that I had no boots and was having to wear clogs all the time. I didn't want to be seen in church wearing clogs, but I was too proud to tell the vicar.

So, to say it was quite an impoverished upbringing would be an understatement, but I had nothing but admiration for my mother. She was a wonderful woman, a real darling. She worked hard at a weaving shed to support us and brought the only useful wage into the house. Naturally, she slowed down as she got older but when I was young she worked extremely hard. She was my first inspiration in life and we remained very close until she died at the age of 82. I'll never forget one thing that she used to say to me. "Thomas," she'd say, as she never called me Tommy, "In life you must learn two things; to give a little and take a little, but give more than you take." It was great advice and I like to think I have followed that throughout my life. I have done well to turn out as I have and a lot of that is down to my mother.

The weekends back in Hindsford with my grandparents used to give me something to look forward to. I would go there every Friday to get away from my father's boozing. Things were certainly different there. Taid's three brothers all lived in the same street and they'd often be round, all speaking Welsh, and the atmosphere was good. It was like being in Wales listening to them all, but none of the language ever rubbed off on me. The only words I picked up were 'nain' and 'taid' and, looking back, perhaps that was a pity. A bit more Welsh in later life might have come in handy for all those clandestine scouting missions I went on for Leigh to rugby union clubs in places such as Bridgend and Cardiff. Believe me, they could smell a rugby league man a mile off down there and wanted you well away from their players. You had to keep a very low profile and try to blend in.

I liked the Sales, although they were a big and complicated family. There were so many of them nearby I never found out exactly how everyone was related to everyone else. There were some cousins there and some of the family were adopted. My dad does not fit into the picture neatly either and I had suspicions that he may have been born out of wedlock. The other members of the family that I saw regularly were my maternal grandparents, the Duttons, who lived just around the corner from Cecil Street on Brunswick Street.

I experienced further tragedy in my childhood when my sister Edith, who was 12 months younger than me, died at the age of 14 from tuberculosis. One family in our street had a history of TB and consequently it swept through the entire row of about eight houses. Only one family escaped. Edith got it on the lungs and quickly deteriorated. It was horrendous. We were great friends and I missed her very much after she passed away. She was such a tomboy, always fighting with the lads. People said she should have been the boy and me the girl. Her death scared me massively. TB was such an infectious and deadly disease and I just didn't want to be in our house. I was frightened to death of coming home at night.

TB struck us again about 12 months later when our younger brother John, who was only a few years old and had shared a room with Edith, caught it. He too was badly affected. I discovered it one night after my mother had asked me to get him ready for bed. I got him to raise his arms so I could lift his jersey off but he screamed out in pain as he did so and his arm dropped. My mother came running to ask what I had done to him. I explained what had happened and when we looked closely we could see one of his shoulders was lower than the other. We had never noticed it before and feared the worst. We called the doctor immediately and John was soon diagnosed as having TB in his shoulder. He went straight to Wrightington Hospital near Wigan and was there for three-and-a-half years. It was heart-breaking. He was a lovely kid and I honestly thought we'd lost him.

But thankfully he pulled through. We used to visit him regularly and it was great when we started to see his strength returning. The treatment they had for him was simply to keep him cold. He used to come running up to us when we arrived, even in the middle of winter, wearing nothing but a little pair of trunks and with a splint on his arm. He used to try to fight with me and we'd have a little wrestle. They were all encouraging signs and he not only survived but went on to become a very good rugby player. When I went to Widnes I took him with me and he soon got into the side at Naughton Park. He was a decent full-back and later represented Lancashire, which is an honour I never achieved. His left arm may have been shorter than his right but he could still catch a ball. He also became a pretty good plasterer too, despite that short arm.

The family was completed by my youngest brother, Frank. I think after my sister died my parents wanted another girl, but another little boy came. Frank also proved a useful rugby player, getting into the Leigh A team. He was as daft as a brush, though. I'll never forget one match he played against Oldham. They had this huge, hulking forward who was a real dirty devil. Before the game Frank said he wanted to sort him out. "I'll finish him, I'll see him off," he said. I told him he was mad. "Frank, if you have any sense you will lay off," I said, but it fell on deaf ears. Frank left the field after the game with a huge black eye. He hadn't half got clobbered! A lesson learned the hard way, I think.

*

Chapter Two

My interest in Leigh rugby club began after we moved within a stone's throw of the ground at Mather Lane. At first I used to take advantage of matchdays to make a bob or two by minding supporters' bikes. A lot of people used to cycle to the game and I'd tell them they could leave them with me. I'd push them into the front garden and get tuppence a time. Sometimes I'd end up with as many as 10, earning me 20 pence. That wasn't a bad return for a Saturday afternoon's work – or at least I thought it wasn't, until my dad came along and took half of the money.

So I suppose that was how my association with the club began, but I soon realised the ground itself was really the place to be. As my interest in rugby grew I started going to watch the games myself and I couldn't get enough of them. I was smitten almost as soon as I'd watched Leigh for the first time and the ground practically became my second home. I used to spend as much time there as I could and became a permanent fixture there in the school holidays.

Chapter Two

I got my first job at Leigh in 1928 when, as a wide-eyed 10-year-old, I was asked by a friend of mine, a lad called Stanley O'Neil, if I could give him a hand operating the scoreboard. Stanley was a keen Leigh supporter whose father Paddy had played for the club before being killed in action during the First World War. He was a little bit older than me and was a familiar face at the club having been asked to be the team's official mascot, in a tribute to his father, when they reached the 1921 Challenge Cup final. I remember seeing a picture from the local paper of both him and his dog wearing Leigh jerseys. I got to know him because he lived close to my grandparents on Brunswick Street. We became quite good friends and he asked me to help out because he knew I lived near the ground.

That is how I first got involved with Leigh. Little did I know then that it was the start of an association that would stretch almost unbroken for more than eight decades.

Operating the scoreboard was great fun. It was a big wooden thing with little metal hooks for numbers we had to change whenever someone scored. The numbers were painted on tin plates and Stanley and I stood at the bottom with a box full of them, watching the game. My appetite for rugby league was well and truly whetted and I knew then that I wanted to play professionally when I grew up. I carried on doing the scoreboard for a few years but stopped at 14 when I first got the opportunity to start playing seriously. The supporters' club had a junior team and I joined it as soon as I was old enough. Playing for them allowed me to pull on a Leigh jersey of some description for the first time and it was a great feeling.

Remarkably, my love for the club was actually fostered during a pretty lean period on the field. Poor performances were not something that ever put me off. Leigh had fallen on hard times since beating Halifax in that 1921 Challenge Cup final at The Cliff, Broughton – the homecoming from which I still have some recollection of – and from finishing fourth in the Championship in 1924.

The two outstanding players of the day were scrum-half Walter Mooney and second row Joe Darwell. They were both good enough to earn selection for a tour of Australia and New Zealand and I remember well watching both of them play at Mather Lane. They were both big characters in the town. Away from rugby they both had pubs and it was outside Darwell's Wagon & Horses, near my Auntie May's house on Norbury Street, that I remember the triumphant cup-winning team pulling up with their silverware. Mooney was also a wrestler in his spare time and once attracted a big crowd to a bout he staged at the rugby ground. He took on a bloke called Paraffin and it was an absolute farce. The pair just had their heads down pushing each other all around the field. It was hardly the entertainment anyone paid for.

Neither Mooney nor Darwell could prevent the decline which saw the club crash to its worst season since formation in 1878 when they finished 24th out of 27 clubs in 1925-26. They failed to win a single match away from home although, along with Featherstone, they played fewer games than anyone else. In those days the Championship was just one division and it was impractical for all clubs to play each other home and away. Instead, all the Lancashire teams played each other twice and the Yorkshire sides did likewise. Some inter-county matches were arranged but some played more than others and so the final table was based on a percentage points system. For fairness, the title was decided by a top-four play-off – so Super League can hardly claim that concept as its own – but that was not something that taxed Leigh. Things got worse in the early 1930s when financial problems began to bite. A number of players were transfer-listed and asked to take a pay cut.

They responded by staging a three-week strike and the club had to field a team of inexperienced youngsters in their place. Attendances declined and there was serious doubt Leigh could continue at one point, a situation that seems to have recurred throughout the club's history ever since. The club survived but it was a precarious existence and there were times when the players had to play for nothing.

But the financial position of the club was hardly something I could claim to know the ins and outs of at the time. I was simply entranced by the game of rugby league, no matter how bad the results. I did joke about it sometimes, however. I used to say they only let me handle the Leigh side of the scoreboard because I couldn't count to more than 10.

Rugby was not my only interest as a child. I used to play a lot of other sports too. I was a very active kid. I found I was quite good at gymnastics and sometimes got asked to take part in displays. I remember being startled one Monday morning when I was called to the front of assembly at Bedford School by my teacher Miss Rose. She was very strict and I wondered what I done to annoy her. I was relieved when she merely said how impressed she had been after seeing me in a gymnastics exhibition at the athletics ground. "I was very proud to see one of our children taking part," she said. "It was a very good display."

I pursued gymnastics until my dad forced me to choose between that and rugby when I was 16. He said I would be an old man before I was 40 if I continued to train at gym three times a week, rugby twice and then play matches at weekends. I was reluctant but, to be fair, it was not the worst advice he ever gave me. It was a simple decision in the end and rugby won. I was a far better player at that than I was a gymnast.

As a child I gave any game a go. I was one of the stars of the school rugby side but the soccer team also took up a lot of my time and I felt I was a pretty useful player in the round-ball code. Tennis was another big hobby while I also liked badminton. I think the only sport I didn't really like was cricket. For some reason it just never appealed to me as much.

I played rugby out of school too. I used to play with friends on the car park of Leigh's Mather Lane ground. It wasn't much of a pitch. It was hard, always covered in ashes and I used to go home with big sores on my arms after diving around and getting tackled. I think I've still probably got ashes in my elbow to this day. I never used to wash them when I got in, I'd just stick a plaster on. A lot of dirt obviously got in because for a long time I had a big mark on my arm. But that was our rugby pitch and I had many a good game there.

I never owned a rugby ball, though, and nor did many of my friends. We simply couldn't afford one. People always managed to get by one way or another, but there really was a lot of poverty in those days. I do remember one boy from my childhood who seemed to have everything but he was very much an exception. He was an only child and was spoilt. The toys he had were unbelievable and I used to spend many hours with him playing with them. He had a rugby ball, a soccer ball and loads of other things besides. He was very lucky and that was certainly not the norm in our neighbourhood.

My background was very modest and when I look back on my life, given such a start, I think it is amazing I achieved what I did in both my rugby and teaching careers. Of course I owed a lot to my wife Evelyne, who was a great help, even though she suffered for it. I was out all the time either at work or the rugby club and she simply never saw me. She actually used to hate Leigh rugby club because it kept me away from her. She reaped the benefits with my earnings from rugby and could afford things she couldn't before but I'll admit I neglected her too much. She claimed it wasn't so much my second home as my first. Things have not changed much in that respect now. I recently had a bit of trouble putting a tie on one morning and put it down to old age. My daughter said she wasn't concerned about it though. “I'll worry when you can't find your way to Leigh rugby club!” she said.

She's probably got a point. I've been finding my way there ever since I got that first job doing the scoreboard. I almost lived there as a kid. I was there just about every day in the school holidays and carried on going until I left at 14 and had to get a job. One of my heroes at the time was a forward called Billy Wood. He was a big lad, a strong, powerful player and I idolised him. He worked at the ground in the week and I used to be there all the time helping him with his jobs, assisting him as much as I could. Even when I was at Bedford School, which was at the top of Mather Lane, I used to nip off every lunchtime and run down the road, over the bridge and into Waterfield's bakery to get his lunch. I'd pick up three meat and potato pies, two for Billy and one for me, and take them to the ground.

It's funny how things turn out. Little could I have known then the impact I and Waterfield's could have had on Leigh. Opened in 1926, that small bakery on Mather Lane was actually the first shop of what became the huge business we know as Waterfield's today. They now have a lot shops across the North West with more planned. The business was set up by Alice Waterfield to feed factory workers during the general strike and was such a success that her husband Albert left his job as a miner to join her. Their children later became involved in the business and their son, Albert junior, became managing director after the death of his father. He oversaw much expansion and, many years later, he and I were among 10 people, also including the Wigan and Great Britain legend Billy Boston, to be awarded the Freedom of the Wigan Borough as part of the Millennium celebrations in 2000. Some eight years after that, when I turned 90, Waterfield's were the obvious choice to do the catering at my party. They did a fine job.

After Mooney and Darwell, my friend Billy Wood was the other great Leigh player of my childhood. I would have loved to have played alongside him. We became firm friends after he took me under his wing as a schoolboy and it broke my heart when he was transferred to Wigan a few years later. Sadly, he only got to play a handful of games for the Cherry and Whites before his career was ended by a horrific injury. It happened in a game against Swinton as he was bending down to score a try. He was just putting the ball down when Swinton's Martin Hodgson, a talented international forward of some repute but a big man and a pretty rough player, jumped on his back. The force bent Billy's knees back the wrong the way and crippled him for life. He was in hospital for a long time and when I went to visit him one of his legs was as black as coal from top to bottom. He was actually lucky not to lose it as the doctors were talking about amputation at one point. Thankfully it never came to that but not surprisingly it was the end of his playing days. Adding to the sadness was the fact that before the accident Billy had been selected to tour with his country. That was a great shame because it was something he really deserved. At least the Rugby Football League still presented with him his touring cap. It is a rare distinction to have been awarded one of those without actually touring, so that was a nice gesture.

Another fine Leigh player to suffer misfortune was a centre called Fred Harris, who came shortly after that era. Fred was spotted playing for Westleigh Recs junior team and was signed up straightaway. He was very fast and a great prospect but Leigh couldn't afford to keep him and sold him to Leeds. That was something that became commonplace. All the top clubs seemed to come and take our best players. Harris was also selected to tour but it came to a premature end after he broke his collarbone in the first match.

One other Leigh player from before the War that I probably should mention was the full-back and captain Tommy Clarkson. He was an inspirational leader, an excellent goalkicker and a great lad.

*

Chapter Three

Leigh was a heavily industrial town in the 1930s. I wonder now what all the people in Leigh do for a living because back then there were so many jobs in industry. I remember four weaving sheds, about six cotton mills, five pits, a tractor plant, a shirt factory, a ladies' underwear factory and Callender's cable works. Between them they employed several thousand people and not one of them is left now. I don't think the population has significantly decreased since, so where have all those jobs gone? Some new businesses have come to take their place but there still aren't many big factories or indeed many large companies in a town that has changed radically, and not necessarily for the better. If you walk down Bradshawgate in the town centre on any given day you do see a lot of people milling about. My guess is many of them are on the dole because the jobs aren't there. It's a shame but Leigh isn't the only place to have suffered such decline. Many other towns are the same.

The mills used to dominate Leigh's skyline and their tall

chimneys were visible from miles away. The rugby league commentator Eddie Waring used to refer to them as the 'Satanic Mills', which was hardly flattering, but did give the town a certain notoriety visiting teams did not like. I think there were as many as 11 mills at one stage and one of them used to overlook the ground at Hilton Park. That one has long since been replaced by an Asda supermarket and only two others are still standing, and they are certainly not operational. The coalmines, of course, have also gone, as have just about all the things that made the North West the industrial power it was.

I got my first job in one of the mills, Parkside, after I left Bedford Church school at 14. I was always destined to end up in work at the earliest possible juncture as I didn't do particularly well at school. I had no encouragement with regards to education from home, mainly because my dad was only interested in his next drink. Had I achieved well I could have gone on to a grammar school but I was nowhere near that level. I spent most of my school years concentrating only on sport. That was all I was interested in and I didn't work hard enough at the academic subjects. I don't remember ever being much trouble, although I did seem to get the cane quite a lot. One teacher, Mr Olive, took a particular dislike to me and it seemed I couldn't go five minutes without crossing him. Still, in the years that followed, I always said corporal punishment never did me any harm. That's why I never had a problem using the stick myself when I became a teacher many years later.

Had I been 12 months younger I might have been able to go on to a new secondary school on Manchester Road after leaving Bedford, as general education for 14-16 year-olds was introduced for the first time. But it was not to be and into the world of work I went, at Parkside mill down Gamble Street.

Mr Rugby Leigh

As the textile industry was so prominent in Leigh I suppose the chances were always high that I would one day end up in a mill. How I wish it could have been different. It was a horrible job and I hated just about every minute of it.

There were two types of mills in Leigh; a spinning mill and what we called a weaving shed, which is where I worked. The spinning mills were the more dominant ones on the horizon at three or four storeys high, whereas the weaving sheds were only one. My task involved sitting on a stool and weaving cotton threads for hours on end. When you finished one job you had to start another. It was incredibly tedious and my loathing of it grew with every shift. As I have mentioned, I was a very active kid and I didn't want to be sitting in a gloomy mill all day every day. I used to go home and cry every night and I dreaded the mornings when my dad used to pop his head round the bedroom door and tell me to get up for work. Some decent pay might have eased my pain but the wages were terrible too. I stuck at it every morning for 12 months and then, by immense good fortune, the mill closed down. To say I was overjoyed would not fully convey my emotion. I could barely contain myself as I left for the last time and threw my cap up into the air.

My relief was short-lived, however, as just a day later a chap who used to work at the same mill popped round to visit. He said there was a job going at a manufacturing company and wondered if I would be interested. It sounded only slightly less monotonous than the mill and I was far from keen. I was just about to tell him as much when my dad suddenly piped up from the next room. Unfortunately he had overheard the conversation and before I'd had chance to speak he'd quickly barked out that I'd be there in the morning. My heart sank. I realised there was no choice and I would have to go.

My father also did his usual worst to add to the misery of this depressing period of my life. One of the few things I got to show for my labours in those two jobs was a nice new bike, purchased after saving hard for £3 17s 6d. That was a significant sum at that time but it was as good as wasted. I did not have the bike long before Dad borrowed it to go to work and came home without it. He was absolutely sozzled and said it had been pinched, but I soon found out that was not true. Someone else told me he sold it for just 30 bob, less than half what I paid for it, and then promptly spent the money gambling. I was very upset.

The second job proved as bad as the first but fortunately I was only there six months before that factory closed down too. That left me unemployed again but, just as before, another job quickly came along and thankfully this time I liked it. It came about through my singing in the choir at Bedford Church. (I'd been allowed back in by then!). I was there one night when one of the choirmasters who had a little soft spot for me and had heard about my redundancy took me aside. He said he knew of a job going in the parks department at Leigh Corporation – the town's administrative entity – and could put a word in for me because he knew the superintendent well. It immediately took my fancy and I said I'd love it. He was as good as his word and it proved just the stroke of luck I needed.

They gave me a job as a gardener at Pennington Hall, which was one of the best maintained parks in the area and is actually very close to where I live now. It was highly enjoyable and did far more than simply keep me off the dole, like my previous positions had. It was very rewarding – although not in a financial sense, and that was not a major concern at the time – and gave me something to look forward to every day. Being out in the fresh air, it was a world away from the dark days in the mill. It was just my cup of tea and I had five good years there until national service was introduced and, at the age of 20, I became one of the first workers from Leigh Corporation to be called up.

The grounds at Pennington Hall were resplendent in those days. The plants we grew were top class and the flower displays were beautiful; thick and full of colour. My foreman and superintendent really knew their stuff. They were excellent gardeners. There was a dahlia border about 30 yards long that people used to come from all over Lancashire to look at. It was lovely, all the coloured dahlia set out in different sections. It was such a pleasant job but, of course, such displays could not be achieved without hard work.

Charlie Gibb, the foreman, was a dour Scotsman who really cracked the whip. He was a stickler for time and you had to be there for 8 o'clock each morning or else there was trouble. As soon as it turned eight he'd start giving his orders and pointing people in different directions. "You: spade, greenhouse," he'd say or, "You: fork, over there." There was no arguing. If you answered back there'd be no second chance. In those days there was a lot of unemployment and nobody could afford to be out of work. Those with jobs were lucky and knew they had to work at them. Charlie demanded high standards and was a hard man to please. If he caught you on your way back to the shed a minute before time there'd be no leniency. "Oi, get back, it's not 12 yet," he'd shout, even if his watch was displaying 11.59.

The main man there was Bill Dyer. He was the superintendent of all the parks in Leigh. He used to live in a house at the top end of the park and had his offices in the hall. He was a lovely man, very considerate, quite the opposite of Mr Gibb. One day, when I was about 16, I was struggling with boils under my arms from an infection. I didn't want to let on but it was painful to dig and Mr Dyer noticed me struggling. He came over to ask what the matter was and so I explained. He took a look and sent me home immediately, telling me not to come back until I was better. Mr Gibb wouldn't have done that, he'd have probably said I had no right to have boils. That infection actually lasted quite a long time and boils were something I suffered from a lot when I was young.

In the winters we used to concentrate on the greenhouses. We grew plants for all the parks around Leigh and produced some wonderful displays. Sadly it is not the same today. Pennington Park, as it is now known because the hall was demolished some years ago, is not maintained as rigorously as it once was. It is still pleasant enough but you'll see something there you never would in Charlie Gibb's day – weeds! He'd be turning in his grave at the thought.

By the time I was called up for national service I was also on the books at Leigh and had become a regular in the first team. My rugby career was developing nicely but the War brought it to a shuddering halt and wiped out six of my best years. I'd been playing seriously since first getting into the Leigh supporters' club team at the age of 14. I actually thought I was one of the worst players in that side and several others seemed more likely to make it as professionals than me, but as it turned out I was the only one that did. I played stand-off for them until I turned 16 and had to look for another team. I then went to play for the amateur rugby club run by Callender's, a huge local firm which manufactured electrical cables, starting in their youth team. Their pitch was actually side by side with Leigh's on Mather Lane so I hardly had far to travel.

I played for Callender's for a couple of years until, by chance, a committee member from Leigh called Fred Prescott walked over the top of the banking to our ground, where we were about to play a game, on the hunt for players. He said the Leigh A side were due to play St Helens A that day and were two men short. He asked our manager if he could borrow a couple of players and mentioned me. The question was then put to me and I had little hesitation. I'd just got changed and was ready to play so it was simply a case of swapping jerseys and walking over to the other pitch. So off I went over the banking with this chap and went straight onto the field to play against St Helens A. I turned out to be one of the youngest in the team but I certainly did something right as they signed me straight after the game.

Leigh were crippled by injuries that season and it was not long before I was given a chance in the first team, playing at centre in a game against York at Mather Lane in December 1938. Unfortunately it was not the most noteworthy of debuts and the report in that week's *Leigh Journal* just about summed it up. "Little was seen of Sale," it read, whilst also detailing how we went down, dismally, in poor conditions, 8-2. It was the first time we had been beaten twice by York in the same season and I don't think the reporter was too impressed.

It was a month before I would trouble him again as I was promptly dropped before the next game. I was recalled for the visit of Widnes on January 14, 1939 and after the previous false start I was determined to make my mark. Widnes at the time were a tough proposition. They were running well in fourth and had put 40 points past us earlier in the season. We were given little hope but I was not the only one fired up and we gave them a real run for their money before losing narrowly 8-5. Considering we played most of the game with 12 men after George Hayes was forced off with a badly gashed head, it was a fine effort and Widnes left knowing they had been in a battle.

It is this game I consider to be the real start of my Leigh career. I was thrown in at half-back alongside Peter Riley and came up against two of the Chemics' most feared players in stand-off Tommy Shannon and scrum-half Tommy McCue. Those two, along with loose forward Harry Millington, had been part of a golden triangle of playmakers that helped the club to three Wembley finals that decade. Shannon knew I was just beginning in the game and went out to ensure I learned the hard way. He ran at me at every opportunity. Perhaps it was the fearlessness of youth, but I was unfazed. I was determined not to let him past and tackled him whenever he came near me with the ball. I was to pay a price as it eventually got to him and he decided to take his frustration out by turning around and flattening me. It was one heck of a clout and there was nothing sly or cunning about it, it was absolutely blatant. Strangely the referee never saw it and, as a skinny kid, I was hardly going to retaliate either, so he got away with it. It was one of a few incidents in a hard-fought game where tempers could be said to have frayed.

It was a tough encounter but I relished the challenge. I never stopped running and should have claimed a try after intercepting a pass but full-back Walter Bradley blocked my kick as I tried to knock it past him. Shannon showed me how it should be done by cutting through our defence for the decisive try as Widnes won. Still, it had been an uplifting game from a personal point of view and I had done enough to keep my place for the next game against Oldham.

The *Leigh Journal* were also rather more upbeat about my performance. "There were some misgivings about playing Sale as Riley's partner, but it must be confessed that, faced with formidable opposition, he made a creditable debut," their report read. That was not only encouraging but also emphasised how forgettable my real debut had been.

As for Shannon, it had been a privilege to see such a master at work at close quarters. I managed to rub him up the wrong way a bit but thankfully he didn't hold a grudge. By the time I joined Widnes myself in December 1949 he had become the coach and we had some very happy times together. I certainly made sure he didn't forget that smack he gave me though. I was always reminding him about it.

I started to feature regularly after that and made nine appearances in total before the end of the 1938-39 season. The Oldham game was actually a chastening experience as we were thrashed 35-2 after losing two players to injury but I celebrated my first try in my next outing against another club I would later represent, Warrington. It was a game memorable for the presence of local boxing hero Peter Kane, who was then world flyweight champion. Kane, one of the greatest fighters of his era, hailed from just a few miles down the road in Golborne and was given a tremendous reception before kick-off at Mather Lane. That made for a great atmosphere but the match itself was a tight affair. My try came when I took a pass from Riley, with whom I was developing a good partnership, and went in under the posts. That ensured the result stayed in the balance for a long time but sadly Warrington hit a purple patch and scored 13 points in the final eight minutes to run out 24-10 winners. Izzy Davies finished with four tries and later went on to end my season by bettering that feat and scoring five against us in a 30-0 thrashing at their place. I was overlooked for the final two games after that.

Nevertheless, despite the struggles of the team, I was reasonably satisfied with my first season of senior rugby. Remarkably, I somehow ended the year with two goals to my name after slotting two between the posts against St Helens Recs. I can't imagine now what must have come over me because throughout the rest of my career I tried to run a mile whenever we needed a volunteer to kick. I simply wasn't very good at it and usually embarrassed myself trying. I'll just put it down to youthful exuberance.

Chapter Three

Although I was obviously happy at breaking into the side, there was no hiding from the club's off-field difficulties. I was well aware that in the couple of years before I signed Leigh had gone cap in hand to other clubs in the hope of loaning players, and had been given permission by the owners of the ground, George Shaw's brewery, to play rent free for a while. I also knew that I'd been given my chance because we were hampered by what turned out to be a record number of injuries. It was not for no reason that we finished 26th in the table.

Unfortunately I had little chance to help put that right as everything stopped for me when I was called up to join the Army on July 17, 1939. Conscription, which had been scrapped in 1919 in the aftermath of the First World War, was reintroduced after 20 years in response to the increasing threat of aggression from Hitler in Europe. When I joined up I was told it would only be for six months and then I would be free to return home. It didn't seem such an ordeal; I wouldn't miss much rugby and Leigh Corporation were obliged to keep my job open for me. But of course I was away for a lot longer than that. War broke out shortly after I was called up and those six months became six-and-a-half years.

I was not quite finished with rugby league, however, or indeed with Mather Lane. I returned home on leave at Christmas in 1939 and made myself available for Leigh's two festive fixtures. They were the only two games I got to play that season, and they both came in the space of 24 hours. Schedules like that weren't something we thought much about in those days. I was keen to show the club what they were missing and scored two tries at Warrington in the first of those games on Christmas Day. Perhaps the Army training had something to do with that as afterwards one of the directors commented on how well I took them and he said he thought I had put on some pace. I then kept my place for the Boxing Day visit of Swinton, which proved to be my last ever game at Mather Lane, my favourite childhood ground. One of my last memories of the place was brushing past my boss, the superintendent from Pennington Hall, and his daughter as I left the field.

The club tried to press on during the War by joining the 1940-41 Lancashire Emergency League but it became an increasing struggle. They played and lost 13 games, all away after losing the use of Mather Lane, and were then forced to withdraw completely after a cup tie in April 1941. I did somehow manage to slip in one game that season whilst on leave before being posted overseas, but after that playing was obviously not an option until I returned home years later.

My appearance in what was a 13-5 loss at Liverpool Stanley made me one of a remarkable 58 players used in just 14 matches, a statistic that clearly illustrates the difficulties the club had. The game itself was a remarkable affair too. Both teams were short of players and it might easily have been called off had Liverpool not somehow found a few more just before kick-off. They eventually managed to field 11 men compared to our 12 and shaded a tight first half 7-5 in wet conditions. The game then changed dramatically in the second half after Liverpool talked an RAF serviceman who had paid his own admission into playing. This man, known only as "Hayes", proved the secret weapon and proceeded to finish us off with two length-of-the-field tries. Unfortunately I had to attempt a penalty at some point in the game too and not surprisingly I missed. Still, the match was a good break from the seriousness of war. When I came back to Leigh several years later the club had all but disappeared. There were few players left and no ground to play on. We effectively had to start from scratch.

*

Chapter Four

The War also meant I had to put my personal life on hold. I'd been courting Evelyne for two or three years when hostilities broke out and we made plans to get married. We managed to squeeze that in in April 1940, shortly before I was sent overseas. Until then I'd been stationed in the UK.

I met Evelyne Briggs in Leigh when I was out on what we used to call the 'monkey run'. This was nothing more than a common walking route from Pennington Hall to the Turnpike Centre in the middle of Leigh but it was how youngsters used to entertain themselves at weekends. It was a good way of getting out and meeting people as there were no youth clubs back then and we certainly couldn't hang out in pubs, like kids do today. Teenagers used to go out and walk up and down the route knowing they could catch up with friends or make new acquaintances.

The girls tended to stick together in groups and I went out with a gang of lads intent on meeting them. Every Sunday night we'd head out and pick up five or six girls and then head back to one of our houses, usually my friend Johnny Jones', for a bit of a party. It was nothing raucous and there was never any drink involved. The lads I used to go out with were Methodists, so that didn't interest them. I met Evelyne one night and took an instant liking. She was a lovely girl with a beautiful head of golden hair. I was determined to see more of her and kept going after her. Fortunately she was always out on the monkey run and the courtship soon began in earnest.

Evelyne was one of four children brought up largely by their mother Jane after their father died young, at the age of about 30. Jane was a remarkable woman and did a fine job for her children. I was so lucky to meet Evelyne. She was immediately so engaging. At the time her family were living in the back of a butcher's shop on Bradshawgate in the centre of town. After that they moved to a council house down Hood Grove and were living there when we got married.

Our wedding took place at Bedford Church and we had the reception for a few family and friends in the Railway pub, near the station. I'd been given three days' leave from where I was stationed in Scotland for the ceremony. After that I had to return to my unit and I was to see her only on two brief occasions before being sent abroad for four years. The first was up at Helensburgh, the Clyde town where we were based for a period. Evelyne came up to visit me for a short time and told me then that she wanted a baby. She said she wanted something to remember me by should the worst happen during the War.

After that I saw her again in Derbyshire shortly before I left the country. We needed to return south to collect new equipment and were sent to a base there. Evelyne was put up in a house and I was able to visit her every night we were there, as long as I was on parade the next day. After that we set sail from Liverpool and it was four long years before I saw my wife again or held my daughter for the first time.

Fiona was born a few weeks after I got on the boat, so it was quite some time before the news caught up with me. I was in Basra, Iraq, when I finally received a brief telegram informing me that I had become a father. "Daughter born, both doing well, love and kisses," it read.

I remember well the first time I saw Fiona. The War was finally being won and I was granted two weeks' leave from my posting in Italy. I travelled home unannounced as there was simply no point writing ahead. It would have taken so long for a letter to have reached Evelyne that I'd have already got home by the time it arrived. By then Evelyne and her family had moved to a little shop in Westleigh and I went straight there, taking the train to Wigan and a bus to Leigh. When I arrived I tried to keep calm and casually walked up to the door and knocked. As luck had it, Evelyne answered and she nearly collapsed when she saw me. "What are you doing here?" she gasped in astonishment. I can still see her expression now.

Fiona ran and hid under the table when I walked into the house. She had no idea who I was. She kept peering out from underneath as this strange man put his arm around her mother. Perhaps she was jealous! It was such a magical moment and Fiona was a lovely girl. It really excited me to see her but sadly it was more than a year after that before I came home permanently. Fiona had a great relationship with her mother throughout her life and I put that closeness down to those years they spent together without me. They developed a special bond. It is so sad they have now both died, but in a way I am at least pleased Evelyne went first. It would have broken her heart had it been the other way round.

I also took the opportunity to visit my old workplace at

Pennington Hall during those two weeks I had back at home. I went in uniform and my boss was very impressed. "What a smart looking fella you are, Tommy," he said. "I'm proud of you." It was great to have that support but missing out on all that home life was difficult. I may have seen parts of the world I would not have done otherwise, and at the Government's expense, but I would much rather have spent that time at home with my family. Readjusting to normal life afterwards was also difficult for many. In more recent times soldiers have come home from the Falklands or the Gulf War after just a few months and been given counselling. There was nothing like that for us, no-one counselled us after six years. We just had to get on with life when we got back.

But I have to say that while the War was a terrible thing, it actually changed my life for the better. It altered my outlook completely and when I returned home I knew I was capable of earning more to support my family than I was working at Pennington Hall. By the end of the War I was a lieutenant and the money was so much better than what I had been used to from Leigh Corporation that I seriously considered staying on in the Army. But, of course, there was no rugby league in the Army in those days and I had a burning desire to restart my playing career. To do that I had to go home, so rugby effectively made the decision for me. I would simply have to find a better job. Yet, were it not for the War, I could easily have been a poorly-paid gardener for my entire working life.

*

Chapter Five

The Second World War was a bloody and tragic affair but I was one of the lucky ones. For some reason I was destined to come through it. A great many people weren't so fortunate and a lot of my friends didn't make it. I endured some horrific moments and saw dreadful things that people should never have to see, but at the end of it I could count myself lucky to have survived. In fact, I was actually doubly fortunate as in the years that followed I believe I actually benefited from the War. I saw a lot of action, travelled the world and was commissioned as an officer. I served in India, the Middle East, Africa, Italy and Germany and I came through the ranks from private to lance bombardier, corporal, sergeant and finally lieutenant. I had a different perspective when I returned after all that and it pushed me into pursuing a career in teaching that served me well for the rest of my life.

I was called up for national service a couple of months before the War and I was actually excited on receiving the initial summons. I thought it'd be a good change, something different and a new experience. Obviously I had no idea then that the minimum requirement of six months' service would be extended indefinitely.

Firstly I had to attend an interview somewhere near Chorley, where I was asked which service I would like to join. I quite fancied myself as a pilot then so indicated a preference for the Royal Air Force, but I was not to get my first choice. I was told to report for basic Army training, with the militia as they called it, in Birkenhead.

I arrived there just a few days before turning 21 and I quickly settled into the camp lifestyle. We did PE every day and as a fitness fanatic I really enjoyed that. I thought it was just up my street. Of course we also did a lot of work on the shooting range, which was just outside Birkenhead, and we spent hour after hour marching, or what we called 'square-bashing'. There was an art to marching together in a column, synchronising your steps. When someone shouted 'about turn' there was a certain drill – left turn, right turn – you had to master. It was hard work and there was one particular day when I really struggled; the morning after my 21st birthday. I'd gone out into Birkenhead the night before to celebrate my coming of age with some of the lads and got absolutely slatted. I was sick on the bus on the way back to the camp. It was a good night but something I soon lived to regret as we were put through our usual drills the morning after.

It was on the parade ground a few months later that we were delivered the news war had been declared. I'll never forget the day, September 3, 1939. It was a beautiful Sunday morning and we were all, about 1,000 of us, under canvas in a field by the woods when we were called out on parade. I think deep down, because of developments in Europe, we all knew there was probably going to be a war but the heart still skipped a beat on being told.

Chapter Five

The whole camp was ordered to line up in front of a big podium on which a colonel stood up in front of a microphone to address us all. He was about 6'7", a really big fella and a smart-looking chap who commanded authority. He stood silent at first for about five minutes, although it felt like five days. You could hear a pin drop as everyone awaited his announcement. Eventually he spoke.

"Men, we are now at war with Germany," he boomed out. "Get digging."

By that he meant dig trenches. No-one really knew how things were going to pan out and so, after the experiences of the First World War, digging trenches to defend the camp seemed a wise course of action. Perhaps they thought the enemy could be parachuted in. So we dug and dug, all around Arrowe Park, which was a base used by the Army throughout the War.

After that we were drafted to units. I was fortunate in that I was to join the Royal Artillery and initially stay in the UK. A great number of the militiamen were sent to units in France for the campaign which ended in hasty evacuation from Dunkirk. I was relatively safe in Scotland when that happened, although I saw some action there too as we attempted to defend German air-raid targets.

Before going up there I was sent to Porthcawl to train on heavy anti-aircraft, or ACK-ACK, guns. We practised by aiming at a huge sock being towed by a plane. We used a predictor to get the target in sight and that then directed the guns and adjusted the metres needed on the range-finder.

The first time I used it in anger was up near Edinburgh after we were sent to defend the Forth Bridge. The Government had feared an attack there and not without good reason, as it proved the target of the Germans' first raid on Britain. We were in position awaiting it but, having not been under attack before, we were not quite attuned to the situation and a little slow to react. We were placed in a field, with guns ready, by a railway station at the south end of the bridge but when the plane arrived we just watched it fly in. Before we knew it bombs were raining down and a ship had been hit, killing some marines. We suddenly awoke to the enormity of the situation and we opened fire, but it was too late. He got away.

From there I was moved on to Glasgow, where I received one of the shocks of my life. I had never heard of groups like the Billy Boys and knew little of the sectarianism that divided a lot of people in that city but I soon found out and it was almost too much to handle. There seemed little untoward as we were allowed a meal in the canteen one Friday night but then suddenly our group divided into two factions, Catholics on one side and Protestants on the other. I hadn't got a clue what was going on and couldn't believe it when they started fighting for little apparent reason. It was quite a battle and I was left totally exasperated. I had never experienced anything like that before and I didn't think I could carry on living among a group like that. At one point I nearly deserted but I resolved to stick with it.

Thankfully I was not in Glasgow too long before being moved west of the city to the lovely town of Helensburgh on the banks of the Clyde. We set up our ACK-ACK guns there too and were kept quite busy by the Germans. The Luftwaffe raided Glasgow while the ship-building ports at Greenock and Clydebank also took a pounding. We had to be on guard for raids all the time. While I was there I also remember seeing a huge ship being towed in along the river. It had a big SOS sign on the bridge and had presumably been rescued from the Atlantic.

During my time in Scotland I revived my ambition of becoming a pilot and actually came close to switching services. There was a shortage of pilots during the first 12 months of the War and I liked the idea of flying a Spitfire, so I put in for a transfer. I went for an interview, got accepted and soon after received a telegram asking me to report to St John's Wood in London prior to embarkation for training in Canada. I got all excited but it was not to be as my major soon put a stop to it.

I'd been in Scotland with the 83rd ACK-ACK regiment for about a year at the time and we'd just heard we were to be posted out overseas. The major insisted I went with them even though I'd been accepted by the RAF. I pleaded with him and told him how much I'd love to train as a pilot but he shook his head. He said he was sorry but I had to go with them. There was no changing his mind. Just prior to that I'd missed out on the week's leave most of the camp had enjoyed as someone had to stay behind to keep guard. I was at least allowed that but then I had to report to Derby for regrouping before setting off. That was the end of any dreams I had of flying Spitfires.

We were to sail out of Liverpool for the Middle East. After a few days in Derby to get kitted out with all the right equipment – we needed new khaki shirts and shorts, as well as other things, for work in hot climates – we set off, taking a circuitous route over Ireland and towards America to avoid U-boats before heading down the Atlantic and into Cape Town to refuel. We arrived in South Africa safely, although I learned a couple of years later how lucky we were to have done so when the same ship, the Viceroy of India, which was an ocean liner adapted for naval purposes, was torpedoed and sunk carrying American soldiers.

We were one of a number of British ships sailing in a convoy around the Cape. Half of us stopped in Cape Town and the rest went a bit further round to Durban. We stopped off for a week or two and saw quite a bit of the place, although there was no time to go up Table Mountain. We refuelled and restocked and then went on to Bombay (or Mumbai as it is now known) for another short stop. That was quite a shocking experience, there was a lot of poverty there and the British weren't very welcome.

I think I was there for about a month before moving on to Iraq, first to Basra and then further north to the RAF aerodrome at Habbaniyah. They had Spitfires and Hurricanes there and ACK-ACK was needed to guard the squadron from attack. We did see a little action there but it was a pretty desolate place. It was out in the desert, west of Baghdad, and there was nothing for miles around. The RAF lot had it slightly better. While we were all out under canvas nearby, they were in lovely billets at the aerodrome and also had their own cinema and theatre at hand. Groups used to come in to put on shows for them. Some of them probably had a great time but for us it wasn't very exciting at all. Thankfully we were only there for about six months before being moved on again, this time to the Iranian port city of Abadan to defend one of the largest oil refineries in the world.

Iran's oil was vital to the Allies during the War and the Abadan plant, owned by the Anglo-Iranian Oil Company, was strategically very important. Its produce came from the oil fields in the north of the country, carried by huge pipelines across the desert. Abadan was an inland port, served by the Shatt al-Arab river, which in turn ran into the Persian Gulf. Tankers would sail up the river and dock alongside huge storage tanks with gasometers to be filled. I think there were about eight or nine of them, such was its capacity.

By this time the Germans were beginning to take a licking in the air and there wasn't as much call for ACK-ACK out in the Middle East. We were not extended much in our time at Abadan and nor were the servicemen there during the rest of the War. The refinery actually came through the conflict unscathed without much alarm, although its importance was highlighted again when it was destroyed during the Iran-Iraq War in 1981. It has since been rebuilt but is no longer Iran's premier refinery.

Fortunately, for us, the town was quite a nice place and there were a lot of English people about. A chap a few of us got friendly with introduced us to a nearby club which boasted a restaurant and we often headed there for our meals. The food was much nicer than that at the Army base. It was there that I first ate curry, and I loved it. Curried prawn has been my favourite meal ever since and now whenever I go to one of my local takeaways they can usually guess what I am going to order.

In both Iraq and Iran I was able to keep my hand in at rugby, playing for our regimental team. It was rugby union of course, a game alien to me, but I enjoyed it all the same. The teams were well organised, the games competitive and the facilities pretty good. Even out in the desert they managed to grow good turf.

The downside to life there was the stifling heat. It was unbearably hot by day. We had to put salt in all our drinking water to stave off sunstroke and it was revolting. Our bodies then used to sweat all that salt out onto our shirts and they would consequently go really stiff when we hung them up to dry. We had to wet them again to get the salt off.

I was actually quite relieved to move on from the Persian Gulf in the end, which came after about six months in Iran when I was recommended for officer training. That was a great moment; I was honoured to be selected. But gaining selection was just the easy part. Attaining the rank of an officer was to prove one of the toughest challenges of my life and thereafter I was to be right in the thick of the action. The intensity of the War was about to increase severalfold and only by luck did I survive.

*

Chapter Six

Major Smith told me to take the jeep after I was summoned from Abadan to Baghdad for an interview the following day with some brigadier or other, with a view to a possible commission. It was quite some distance across the desert, more than 300 miles, so I packed my bags and set off. I saw the brigadier and passed the interview. He said he would be forwarding my name to the Officer Cadet Training Unit in Acre, Palestine, and I would hear from them in due course. Two or three weeks later, back in Abadan, Major Smith summoned me again and told me I had been accepted. He told me I had to report to Acre the following week. To get there I had to get back to Baghdad and then cross Syria and a lot more desert. The major sent me with a driver for the first part of the journey and then I had to get a coach all the way to Acre.

What followed were six of the most exciting but toughest months of my life. I was always willing to meet challenges but it was far, far from easy at the OCTU. The sergeants there were all officious, offensive, obnoxious types who were very strict and treated you like dogs. They did everything they possibly could to try to break you and if they succeeded you were out, not deemed fit enough to be an officer. But they couldn't break me. I was fit, very fit, and equally determined. I took everything they threw at me.

They used to order us to do all kinds but it never bothered me. I could handle the assault courses, carry anything they asked and could run all day. As a rugby player I always took pride in my reputation as one of the fittest players on the field and I was just as driven in my Army days. I looked after my health, didn't smoke and it helped that I played in the unit's rugby team, of which I was one of the stars. I was also disciplined in the face of provocation. The sergeants used to come up to you calling you all names under the sun, sometimes thrusting their noses right up to yours. They would implore you to respond and try to expose weaknesses but you had to keep still and take it. Even if you so much as blinked at the wrong time you were out.

It possibly helped that I got friendly with some of the Kiwi and Aussie soldiers that were there. For some reason our Antipodean comrades were always treated a bit more leniently and never got thrown out. An example of this was when we were out on parade one morning and they were barking out orders to various individuals in the line.

"Come up in the middle, come back in the middle, move up at the end," one sergeant bawled, repetitively, seemingly singling out one particular Aussie more than anyone else. Eventually it got to him and he bit back, stepping out of the line and shouting, "For Christ's sake make up your mind!"

The guards immediately grabbed him and yanked him out of the line, but he wasn't banished like one of us Brits would have been. We'd have been returned to unit – RTU'd as we called it – for sure. He got away with a week under guard. So it came in handy to make friends with some of the guys from Down Under and, as a lot of them liked their rugby too, I found them an easy bunch to get along with.

Without friends like that carrying me through I'm not sure I would have made it. More than once I wondered whether it was really worth it because of how difficult it was. Yet I stuck at it and eventually earned the rewards as I was commissioned and left as a second lieutenant. From then I was transferred from ACK-ACK to Field Artillery and informed I was to be "sent up the blue" or, in other words, deployed close to the front line in the north African desert. I was to join up with the 83rd field regiment, who were a well established force from Kent and ironically bore the same number as my old ACK-ACK regiment. They had all been territorials before the War and were effectively all pals together, though, which meant my promotion prospects were not great. I did manage to move up to lieutenant but all the positions of captain after that had been filled so, unless anyone got killed, I knew I was unlikely to go higher.

Before I joined them, however, those of us that came out of the OCTU were allowed a little rest and recuperation after a gruelling six months by being allowed a fortnight's leave in Cairo. How we enjoyed that! Being commissioned was one of the greatest moments of my life and I, like the others that achieved it, wanted to celebrate. We did our best to paint Cairo red. There was plenty of drink and other such off-duty shenanigans, although I think most drew the line when it came to women, despite temptation. I don't think you could be safe getting into bed with anyone there. There was too much to lose and no-one wanted to risk getting VD! I didn't hear too many stories of that sort of thing going on but we all did the sight-seeing essentials of visiting the pyramids and Sphinx. It was a great couple of weeks but it was only a brief respite from the harsh realities of war.

Chapter Six

Soon enough I was thrown right into the thick of the North African Campaign. For three years in total the Allies and the Axis powers chased each other back and forth other across hostile desert terrain, each side taking it in turns to push the other back. For the Allies, north Africa represented a route back into western Europe after the fall of France whilst the Germans and Italians wanted to get through Egypt to take charge of the Suez Canal and the oil fields of the Middle East.

There had already been a number of attacks and counter-attacks, the Allies trying to push out west from Egypt and the Germans looking to advance eastwards from Libya, when I first became involved in the campaign early in 1942. The Allies fighting in north Africa were collectively operating as the Eighth Army. I joined up with my field regiment during a period of retreat and we were pushed back to El Alamein, just west of Alexandria in Egypt, where two ferocious battles ensued. The first, in July 1942, managed to halt the German advance and we were able to regroup. Hostilities broke out again three months later as we launched a fresh offensive. We were told this was it, that we could not retreat any farther back into Egypt. We had to stand our ground and basically fight until the last of us was standing. The cost of failure was enormous because allowing the Germans into Alexandria would have effectively ended the North African Campaign.

My task in the artillery was to operate guns known as the 25-pounders. We used to refer to them as the pea-shooters for the infantry, who marched ahead of us, and I found it much more exciting than ACK-ACK. I had not fired a shot in anger for ages in ACK-ACK, indeed we used to spend most of our time cleaning the guns, but this was a different game altogether and I was initially glad of the change. I used to say it was more like duck shooting, with the obvious difference that they could fire back at you. It goes without saying that being under fire was not a nice experience.

The Eighth Army by this time was under the command of the charismatic General Bernard Montgomery, who went on to become one of the heroes of the War. He was very efficient and an inspirational leader. All the officers were scared of him and he would shut them up in no time if they weren't doing their job. Obviously I was much farther down the line and never had to deal with him personally, but the message was clear. If he said jump, you jumped.

Prime Minister Winston Churchill later referred to the second battle of El Alamein as one of the major turning points of the War. When we were pushed back we were a dispirited force but we started to 'barrage' them and it worked, allowing us to strike back. Basically, all the artillery had to line up side by side and fire at their front line. We had so many 25-pound guns that I think our line stretched across for about two miles.

The assault started one night with the first barrage shots. Every gun fired as many shells as possible to saturate their front line. As soon as they started retreating we were to advance and then repeat the barrage. We called it leap-frogging and it was successful. We kept on pounding the Jerries and chased them all the way back along the north African coast to Tripoli. They fired plenty back at us, of course, and that was very frightening but we held the upper hand, captured a lot of prisoners and eventually forced their retreat into Italy.

I saw some horrible and very upsetting things along the way. With the artillery I was part of the follow-up force rather than the invading force, the infantry. As we swept through the desert or the occasional town behind them the aftermath of the bloody battles was always all too evident. There were bodies strewn everywhere. Somehow you managed to desensitise yourself when you saw German corpses lying there but seeing your own was sickening. After we got to Tripoli I was given the job of getting a lot of them cleared up and buried. It was one of the most horrendous experiences of the War. It was something I will never, ever forget and it changed my life. I tried not to take much for granted after that, although at the time I quickly had to put it out of my mind. War does that to you, it is an inhuman thing. You can't afford to act or think like a human being. If you do, you go down.

The Eighth Army was to maintain the offensive and follow the Germans into Italy, but first a lot of us were sent back to Alexandria to regroup and collect fresh equipment. I had not been back there for long when I was told to briefly return to Tripoli for a course. To save time I was sent by sea on a ship called the Erinpura. I was not detained long and was then sent to join a unit at Benghazi and lead an overland convoy back to Alexandria.

It was during that journey that one night I received another reminder of how precarious life was during the War. I had decided that we should set up camp for the night, or 'laager up' as we called it. We all pitched our tents in a circle around a fire and were cooking all sorts of tinned food in our big pots when we noticed a jeep approaching us from the distance. It drove up to us and an officer stepped out, asking if he could laager up for the night with us. I told him he was most welcome and invited him to have some food with us. He said he too was heading for Alexandria and then told me he had just had a narrow escape. He said he had come off a boat, the Erinpura, that had just been sunk in the Mediterranean and he was one of few survivors. His words cut like a rapier. I was shocked and not for the first time I realised how lucky I was to be alive. I told him I'd sailed on that ship without mishap just a couple of weeks earlier. Dryly, he said that was something I wouldn't be doing again because it was now at the bottom of the Mediterranean. It was the second ship, after the Viceroy of India, I had been on that had gone down.

The sinking of the Erinpura by the Luftwaffe just off Benghazi in May 1943 was a major British naval disaster. The hatch had been open and one plane hit it with a single bomb that went straight through and out of the bottom. The whole ship sank in about five minutes with a loss of 943 lives, although there are conflicting reports of the exact figure. More than two thirds of those killed were soldiers from the British African colony of Basutoland, which is now Lesotho, the country landlocked by South Africa. The officer was one of only 273 that survived. Most of those killed had been below deck because everything happened so quickly and there was no way out. I'd spent a lot of time in the lower decks when I was aboard and thought nothing of it. Two of the Basotho men, however, actually had a remarkable escape. They were trapped beneath but luckily for them the rising water compressed the air and forced a ventilator open. They were able to get out onto deck and were rescued.

After that it was back to Alexandria and then on to Italy, which of all the countries I visited during the War was the one I liked the most. It was some time before I could enjoy its natural beauty as there was some serious fighting to be done first but the war gradually began to thin out as we worked our way up the Adriatic coast, over the course of two-and-a-half years, from our landing point at Taranto. We went through towns such as Brindisi, Bari and Rimini as we made our way north, finishing at Trieste. Sometimes we were detained for a week or two as we got the better of the opposition but the tide generally went in our favour and we could take in a bit of Italy as we got towards the end. We were in Trieste, right in the far North East, when we heard the War had ended and the vino certainly flowed that night.

Chapter Six

Operating the 25-pounders in Italy was again risky business and the most dangerous part of it entailed working in observation posts (OPs). Tactics had to be different from the desert and we had to create OPs wherever we could, often whilst right in the front line with the infantry. Those in the OPs were responsible for directing guns onto targets.

In a few towns we discovered that cemeteries made good OPs as they often had little chapels you could conceal yourself in and knock a little hole in a wall to spy through. We found one though that had been completely desecrated and it was quite a sad sight. In the chapel were a number of coffins piled on top of each other on either side. It was probably a family vault. There were marble slabs at the end with pictures of the occupants but they had all been opened with skeletons scattered everywhere. It was awful and we presumed people had done it to steal rings off fingers. A little while later I remember shielding behind the wall in this chapel, overlooking a valley, when I heard a voice saying, "Here have a biscuit, here have another biscuit." I looked round and my signalman was throwing biscuits at the jaw of a skull in the corner. It was very black humour indeed. We encountered another couple of chapels that had been similarly bashed up after that. It was a shame because they were lovely little buildings.

OPs were dangerous places. You had to stay concealed and keep activity to a minimum during daylight or risk being bombarded by the enemy artillery. Yet we had a vital role to play. On one occasion south of the river Po we were asked by the infantrymen to put a 'stonk' on a farmhouse. This meant firing all guns at once to destroy a single target. Each regiment had four batteries of four guns and on this particular day I was in the OP in charge of directing them. When preparing to stonk you first fired one gun for ranging. You'd try to work out the distance on a map and, for example, maybe fire one gun 1,600 yards. If it dropped short of the target you'd then increase the distance being fired to maybe 1,800 or 2,000 yards. If it then went over you could then come back halfway in between. This was called bracketing and when you were satisfied you'd then call for the four-gun fire.

The infantry had said every time they got close to this farmhouse, which was right by the river, they got shot at. We fired our stonk at it in daylight. The first round dropped short and the next a bit over, then the third fell right on it. The result was incredible. What an explosion. The whole thing blew sky high! Men with clothes alight came running out and jumping into the river. We'd only managed to hit an ammunition dump with a direct hit. It was a lucky sight because it was well guarded, but those guards soon left it when it went up!

Whilst there was some excitement and satisfaction in scoring such a hit, it did not usually last long. War was not a game and it was very frightening. The enemy stonked us a number of times and I was so scared some nights that I wet my bed more than once. I remember one such time was after another very narrow escape.

We were out in a village and the men who had been in charge overnight had dug a trench in a field to shield from any flying shrapnel whilst they tried to get some sleep. I was sent by the captain to go and check on them but just as I was about to walk around the corner of a building I heard a huge explosion and saw water gushing everywhere. A shell had struck the van carrying our drinking water tank. Another second and I'd have been round that corner and would have gone up with it. When I returned to the captain I was shaking like a leaf. He asked what was wrong and I said I'd show him, but he realised that wasn't necessary.

I remember another near miss when we were getting

stonked in broad daylight. We took cover but one captain left his post. We told him not to go because we were still being fired at but he still went. A few minutes later we saw him lying on the deck with no obvious signs of anything untoward having happened. We soon realised he was dead but we could not work out what had happened. There was no blood or clear wound. Only on closer examination did we notice a small spot on his head, no bigger than a quarter of an inch. A tiny piece of shrapnel had got into his brain and killed him. You were really never safe. He might have survived had he gone out with his helmet on rather than his cap and that was a warning to us. Our helmets were a bit of a nuisance, not nearly as good as the ones the Germans had, which were big and quite protective. They were not well designed and at times you did forget to put them on, but that was a silly thing to do.

Tragically, I saw so many young lives cut short, and not always through direct fighting. I remember with great sadness how another of our number met the most unfortunate of ends. He was such a popular lad who gave everything for the cause. He relished working in the observation posts and was always volunteering to go up there. That job was highly dangerous and we were all supposed to take our turn on a rota, but he was always offering to cover other people's slots. He was fearless. When the War ended we were all allowed to take convalescent leave in turn. We decided to vote for who should go first and it was unanimously agreed that he deserved it most. A special sight-seeing trip to Rome was being arranged and he was quite keen to go, so we made sure he was free. Unbelievably, he was then killed in a road traffic accident. After everything he had been through and done for us, it was such a waste. The news really broke us and there was not an officer with a dry eye when we heard. It was such a shame.

It was always hard to deal with death and it seemed especially wasteful when people died in accidents, not as a result of combat. I buried two lads in Brindisi after they drowned swimming in the sea. We'd given ourselves a bit of space and gone down to the sea for a dip but they got into trouble and the current took them out. There were a lot of soldiers laid to rest out in Italy but I can remember clearly to this day where I buried them.

Yet for all the bitter memories I have of Italy, I do have some good ones as well. Apart from the first Christmas we were there, when it snowed and the locals blamed us for bringing such freak weather, the climate was superb and as we moved on we began to enjoy a bit of the country. There were a lot of nice towns and the orange groves and vineyards were fantastic. They were huge and we used to just walk in and help ourselves to lots of juicy, ripe fruit, although we upset the odd farmer or two doing so. There was also plenty of good wine in Italy and we didn't waste much when we got the chance to drink some.

I took it upon myself to learn Italian and I became quite fluent. Fraternising with the locals was not so much frowned upon as outright forbidden, but I did do a very little when it was safe to do so. I had worked too hard for my commission to put my pips in jeopardy by taking unnecessary risks but on the odd occasion I did get out to put my Italian into use. It was such a beautiful language and not too difficult to learn. You can pick up more in six months when you're out in a country than you can in six years at home with a book. I was very cautious but sneaked in some practice whenever I could and enjoyed chatting here and there. I tried to keep it up in the years that followed too and went back to Italy for family holidays a number of times. I still speak a little now, although I've forgotten a lot of it.

I got the chance to see the artwork of Florence, the wonders of Rome and the canals of Venice. The thing I remember most about Venice, however, was the fish. I ordered some in a restaurant and the ones that were served up were ugly things about three or four inches long with eyes still in them. You had to eat the lot. It was enough to put me off fish for a while.

We were also in Italy during the last great eruption of Mount Vesuvius in 1944. We were near Brindisi on the Adriatic coast, the opposite side of the country, when it occurred but the ashes and sulphur still reached us. I remember looking out to see this big black cloud coming over and settling on the fields. The farmers loved it and they rushed out to plough it in.

In some towns we enjoyed a little comfort by occupying houses and at one place just north of Rimini we took over a farmyard. We thought we'd done well when we found a big vat there full of wine but it soon became apparent there was a horrible smell emanating from it. Consequently we wouldn't touch it and we thought the Polish troops based nearby were mad to keep coming through and happily fill their bottles. Eventually we decided we had to investigate and our suspicions were confirmed when we opened it up and found a dead German floating in it. He probably hadn't been dead that long but it was long enough for him to stink the place out and his flesh was like jelly. And the Poles had been drinking the wine! It made you sick just thinking about it. I'm so glad we never went near it.

One night when we did drink plenty of wine, however, was after we heard the War was won. We were just outside Trieste when we received the news. It was a fantastic moment but there was no quick return home. We still had a lot of prisoners of war and we were sent back to a camp at Rimini to guard them. At least by this time I had become the longest-serving overseas soldier in our regiment so when it next came to granting leave home, I knew I was top of the list.

*

Chapter Seven

It was magnificent to finally come home for the first time after the War but my joy was short-lived. I was granted two weeks' leave to see my family but had not been back long when I received a telegram informing me it had been extended by a week prior to embarkation for Germany. I couldn't believe it. I'd spent most of the War overseas and now they wanted to send me abroad again to guard prisoners of war. It didn't seem fair. I couldn't understand why some of the servicemen who had never left Britain during the main years of fighting, and there were a lot of them, were not getting chosen. Instead, it was my sort again. But mine was not to reason why. I had no say in the matter and I had to go. I reported to the Royal Arsenal in London and was told I would be sent to a POW camp at Wuppertal.

This proved a dicey assignment to say the least. All the prisoners were SS men and they were right nutters, especially the officers. I'd come across them before at the camp in Rimini, where we had held about 3,000 of them.

That camp had been about two miles inland and we regularly had to transport them to the seaside, under armed guard, to let them swim and get clean. We took them about 30 at a time and that was a lot to handle because they were so volatile. They also turned on each other and quite a few times, despite watching them carefully, we found bodies floating in the water after one had drowned another. It was as if they were meting out their own kind of justice for any kind of altercation back at the camp.

In Wuppertal we housed them in Nissen huts, which were semi-cylindrical cabins made of steel, all built in a line. They are quite common on Army camps. There were about 15-20 men in each hut and we wouldn't dare go into one to see them on our own. There had to be three or four of us with rifles cocked at the ready, because these men were dangerous and daft enough to have a go. It wouldn't be exaggerating to say they'd have slaughtered a single soldier entering. We also had several more cases of them killing each other while we were there and a number of suicides. The outside perimeter of the camp was a tall fence but inside that there was another fence, just a few feet high, which they were not allowed to cross. If any of them stepped over it the guards in the tall sentry boxes had to shoot them. These men deliberately used to step over with their arms up, challenging our guys to shoot, which of course they had to do. They were absolutely crackers the SS, a terrible lot to deal with – but a tough nut to crack.

Outside of the camp I found the Germans a cold and arrogant people. Whereas I enjoyed meeting the Italians and found them friendly, the Germans were very different. We did not fraternise with the locals and stuck to our own. We found plenty of ways to enjoy ourselves during downtime but, for me, the main thing was rugby. After the intensity of the final few years of the War, getting out on a field again with a ball in my hands was wonderful.

*

Chapter Eight

I knew little about rugby union when I joined the Army. The game was barely on my radar as I grew up in Leigh, where rugby league overshadowed all other sports. I soon realised that would have to change if I wanted to carry on playing the oval-ball game in some form because rugby league was non-existent in the armed forces. There was a lot of animosity between the codes in those days and union, boasting a multitude of Army officers in lofty positions, was the game of the Establishment. There was simply no way league, perceived as a rival upstart code from working-class northern England and sneered at by the rulers down south, could ever get a look-in. Only in relatively recent history has this changed. It was not until 1994 that rugby league was finally recognised formally by the armed forces and only since then have units been able to form teams. Now sides from the Army, RAF and Navy compete in the Challenge Cup each year and that represents real progress.

So I took up rugby union and enjoyed it from the off. I

became an instant hit because, to be honest, I found it easy. It was not as fast a game. I liked to run with the ball and the union players, too used to kicking, did not know how to handle me. Outside of the forces, anyone who had played rugby league, at any point, was forbidden from playing rugby union. That rule did not apply inside the Army and there have been many stories of rugby league players excelling in the other code whilst in the services, but I kept my allegiances fairly quiet at the time. It was not worth the hassle of telling anyone where I learned my game.

I played fly-half for my regimental team whilst we were stationed at Habbaniyah in Iraq and at Abadan in Iran. The pitch in Iraq was absolutely brilliant. Its lovely green grass was so striking amid all the sand of the desert. It was adjacent to the river Tigris and they used to flood it every day to maintain its lushness. I played so well in one game there against the RAF that I was tapped up by the opposition in the bar after the game. The squadron had a game against another Army unit coming up and they wanted to sneak me in as a ringer. Not being one to turn a game down, I agreed willingly but I was rumbled on the day. I drew attention to myself by having another blinder and scoring a couple of tries and the Army lot couldn't believe it afterwards when they saw me back in the bar in one of their uniforms. I got plenty of stick for that but it was all good natured. One thing I was justifiably lampooned for however was my goalkicking. For some reason no-one volunteered to kick after one of my tries and as I had the ball in my hand I had to have a go myself. I sliced it horribly wide and vowed there and then never to attempt it again.

After leaving Iraq I played at the Officer Cadet Training Unit in Palestine and featured in a representative side against a team of Kiwi soldiers. As I moved on to Africa, however, rugby was very much forgotten. It was not until after the War and when I arrived at the POW camp in Germany that I was able to take it up again. After everything that had gone on, that was a source of great enjoyment for everyone. We established a strong team at our Wuppertal base and played many good games there against other regiments. It was also whilst in Germany that I enjoyed two of the highlights of all my rugby-playing days.

After the War, the commander of the Second New Zealand Expeditionary Force, General Freyberg, decided to set up a team from men who had served in Europe, Africa and the Middle East to tour Britain, France and Germany in 1945-46. He was a huge enthusiast for the game and had sought to arrange matches for his men at various times throughout the War. His venture attracted much interest and, after meeting hundreds of hopeful players, he built a formidable squad after a series of rigorous trials.

Only one of the team, Major Charlie Saxton, had previously represented the All Blacks but the talent on show was phenomenal and 16 of the 31 chosen eventually went on to play for their country. They played Tests against England, Scotland, Wales and France and established a reputation for entertaining rugby. They won 29 of their 33 matches during the tour and such was the excitement generated that they had to arrange more matches when they returned home to appease the locals.

There was much anticipation when we heard they were to come through Germany towards the end of the tour and play matches against the British Army of the Rhine and the Combined Services. Naturally I wanted to play in both and did so after impressing in the trial matches.

In the final trial match for the BAOR team I lined up at stand-off opposite an officer whom, word had it, was a strong rival for my position. He was a major who had played for the Scotland national side and was supposedly a very good player. Much to his disgust, however, I completely outplayed him to win selection. The thing I never understood about rugby union was why players seemed to scrap like hell in the ruck to win the ball only for the acting-half to pass it to someone to kick. That was all this major did. Every time he got the ball he kicked it. That was nonsense to me and I did not want to get involved in that game. I wanted to run with it and did so at every opportunity. When I got the ball I'd sidestep them and beat them. It opened the game up and caught the eyes of the selectors. Apparently the Scottish major was very upset afterwards and couldn't believe he'd been beaten but all I did was play my natural game. I similarly got the better of an Ireland international in one of the other trial games too. After winning selection I was joined in the team by another rugby league player in Jimmy Stott, who later enjoyed a fine career with St Helens.

Both games against the Kiwis were memorable occasions and they did not run rings round us, like everyone expected. We gave them a good run for their money. I was stand-off in both games, the first of which, for the BAOR, was played at Wuppertal and the second, for the combined Army, Navy and RAF team, at Hamburg.

We lost the Wuppertal match 12-0 before being taken to Dusseldorf for a great after-match party. Apparently the Kiwis were to be treated as ambassadors with no expense spared, so the organisers booked the yacht club and bought in 200 bottles of champagne and two barrels of beer. It was a similar affair in Hamburg after the next game, in which we were also beaten 20-3.

One thing that stands out from that game, played at the Bahrenfeld Stadium, was the kicking of a player I'd obviously never heard of called Bert Cook. He landed two penalties, one of them an extraordinary effort after I was penalised on the halfway line. As soon as the whistle went our captain, who was a lieutenant colonel, started berating me, saying how foolish I'd been and claiming I should have known Cook would kick it from there. I didn't really believe him and said: "Sir, if he can kick it from there he deserves it."

I walked back and positioned myself in the middle, in front of the posts, expecting his effort to drop into my arms well short of goal. Cook, their full-back, was only about 5'3", as broad as he was tall and wearing size three boots. I had never seen a player with such small feet and didn't think he had any chance of kicking it. Yet he struck it absolutely perfectly and I watched in amazement as it sailed over me. It was still going up as it went over the posts.

I got chatting to Cook at the meal after the game and he asked me which club I played for back home. I told him I didn't play rugby union and that I played rugby league, although I tended to keep that quiet. As a result, the hostility between the codes was not something I experienced much. Cook's ears immediately pricked up and he asked me more. Speaking in hushed tones, he told me he'd had an approach from Leeds and was giving serious consideration to turning professional with them. They'd spotted him earlier in the tour. He asked for my advice and I told him simply that he could not go far wrong by joining Leeds. They were one of the best clubs in the country and were very well run off the field.

Cook took my word for it and joined Leeds the following year. He was an instant success and went on to become a club legend, scoring 556 goals in 210 appearances for the Loiners. He played at Wembley in his first season and it was hardly a surprise to me that he kicked one goal during that cup run from inside his own half in rain and thick mud at Wigan. He was a fearsome competitor, a strong-running full-back and a bruising tackler but it was his kicking that impressed me most. I have never seen anyone who could direct the ball as he could. He could make it swerve to the right or left and his touch kicking was also immaculate. He could land it on a threepenny bit. The only kicker that came close for me was Jimmy Ledgard, the legendary Leigh full-back. He too could land it wherever he wanted and that is the hallmark of a great kicker. Both Cook and Ledgard were brilliant in the days when full-backs used to engage in kicking duels, both looking to force each other back or find touch. It was a big part of the game then but you don't see much of it now. The pair also used to kick goals for fun.

Cook and I became good friends after that and we'd always have a chat whenever our paths crossed. He became player-coach at Keighley and later Dewsbury after leaving Leeds but sadly he died young from cancer.

The significance of the tour by the 2NZEF is not lost in books on the history of rugby union. The team acquired a popular following and became known as 'The Kiwis' as they travelled around rather than the All Blacks, which was the nickname of the full national team. The tour helped repopularise the game both in Europe and in New Zealand after the War and it was great to have played a small part in that. In fact, I had a lot of good games of rugby union in the Army and I look back on them with great affection. They were happy days. That said, I was glad to get back to rugby league when I returned home permanently after 12 months in Germany. I missed it a lot and I didn't really follow rugby union much thereafter. It just didn't interest me. Rugby league is a faster game and much more challenging to play. There are more gaps because there are only 26 men on the field but you need pace and power, the two Ps, to get through. Pace in the backs and power in the forwards are the two essentials you need to succeed in rugby league and it was good to get back to playing a game where that mattered.

Yet my rugby union career did not completely end then as there was a postscript a couple of years later when I was called up for emergency 'Z training'. Shadows were looming over Europe again and the Government wanted to keep men in shape in case the Cold War escalated. I rejoined an ACK-ACK regiment for three weeks' training on the south coast at Weymouth, work which mainly involved firing at an airborne sock again. While there we set up a regimental team to play a few games and I was lucky enough to get put together with a group of territorials from Wigan, all rugby league lads. In one game we played against a Welsh regiment and really took them to the cleaners. They wanted to play the kicking game but we played the attacking game and there could only be one winner. Happy days.

*

Chapter Nine

Life was never the same for me after the War. I could grumble about how I was robbed of six-and-a-half years of my youth but I won't. I feel very lucky to have survived and I have said that many times. I also feel my war years made me the man I am. You could never escape the true brutality of what was going on and it was often hard to take, but in the face of adversity I experienced some exciting times and great comradeship. Becoming an officer also toughened me up and that experience of responsibility and dealing with people spurred me into seeking a better career path to the one I was treading back in 1939.

I was a mere gardener when I joined the Army and I came out as a lieutenant. That was quite a promotion and the difference in the pay between the two jobs reflected that. When demobilised and faced with a return to my old job at Pennington Hall or staying on in the Army, I was initially 50-50 over what to do. It would obviously have been nice to go home but I had to consider the fact that I only ever earned

£3-4 per week from Leigh Corporation, whilst in the Army I was pocketing £15-20 per week. Even that was a rise on the 30 shillings or so I was on when I started. I had to decide what was best for me and my family.

In the end rugby league was the decisive factor. I wanted to go back to Leigh and start playing again and I could not have done that in the Army. Had I stayed on I could have been based anywhere and playing opportunities would have been limited to the 15-man code. So I decided to go back to Pennington Hall, as the job had been kept open, although no matter how much I might have enjoyed it I knew it was not something I could countenance for long. I would simply be underselling myself. I had to keep an eye open for new opportunities and, with that in mind, I thought it best to pick up my education. During my time in the Army I studied a lot of mathematics because of all the gunnery involved and I found it very useful. I thought I could put that to use again and decided to brush up and improve by undertaking a correspondence course in the subject. To complement it I also did one in English. As a schoolboy all I'd concentrated on was sport. Now I realised the importance of an education.

As for the rugby, there was none initially at Leigh but I was fortunate enough to be able to start playing again almost as soon as I returned. That was because – and not a lot of people these days realise this – I had reached an agreement to turn out for Warrington.

That was something that had come about quite by accident whilst on a short leave from the prisoner of war camp in Germany. A friend of mine called Harry Bond, who was a good amateur player for Astley & Tyldesley, was also running a team in Culcheth at the time. When he heard I was back in Leigh he came round to see me and asked if I fancied a game. His side were due to play Warrington A and needed a stand-off. I agreed and he said I wouldn't regret it because he'd found a very good scrum-half to play alongside me in someone named Gerry Helme. Harry was as good as his word as Helme was an absolute belter. We hit it off straightaway and had a brilliant game together, so much so that as soon as it finished a Warrington delegate came over wanting to sign us both.

Warrington were putting a new team together and we were both very keen. I certainly saw it as an excellent opportunity to ensure I had a professional club waiting for me if or when I left the Army. At the time there was no certainty rugby in Leigh would ever be revived. Not only had the team been decimated but the ground had also been sold and it was obvious it was going to be some time before things got up and running again, if ever. I thought it best to grab what Warrington were offering while I could.

It was not a decision I dwelt on long and both Gerry and I were at Warrington later that day to sign. We discussed signing-on fees between ourselves beforehand and I decided that I was going to ask for £100. I thought it was a reasonable amount and I was cheered when Gerry, who went into the office first, came out laughing. He had obviously been given the money he wanted. I don't know what he asked for but I stuck to my figure of £100 and couldn't believe it when they agreed without hesitation. My eyes lit up as, with barely a moment's thought, someone opened up a box and handed over the cash. It seemed like my lucky day – but then I went and opened my mouth.

"Does it not matter if I signed for Leigh before the War?" I asked. I'd hardly finished the question before the same person had leant over and snatched the £100 back out of my hands. I couldn't sign for Warrington because I was still on the books at Leigh. Even though the club were not operating at the time, my registration was still with them and I remained their player. That was a blow but there was a consolation. Because of Leigh's inactivity I was still free to play for Warrington as a guest until such a time as my parent club did get started up again. That was something I was happy to do and I did turn out seven times for the Wire in the 1945-46 season, scoring one try.

I first played for Warrington when I returned home on leave in October 1945, featuring in defeats against Broughton Rangers, when I seem to remember being given a tough time by their stand-off, and Barrow. I then returned to Germany and it was not until towards the end of the season, after I played those memorable Army games against New Zealand, that I got another chance.

My one try in Warrington colours could hardly have been more dramatic, it settling a Good Friday derby at Widnes in the closing minutes. The game itself was a pretty dour affair but we battled on and I forced my way over to snatch a 7-5 win just before the final whistle. Dave Cotton, one of the great hookers of his day, rushed over and rubbed my hair vigorously in relief and celebration. It wasn't the only good game I ever had against Widnes and I wonder if someone had remembered that when I came to sign for them a few years later.

I managed another handful of games for Warrington, all at half-back, before it began to look like Leigh could be back in action by the start of the 1946-47 season. A very ambitious chap called James Hilton had arrived on the scene with a fierce determination to get the club restarted. That was something that really excited me and I was keen to be involved, but there was still a tinge of sadness at leaving Warrington. I enjoyed my time there playing alongside the likes of Cotton, Harold "Moggy" Palin, Albert Johnson and, of course, Gerry Helme. Unfortunately I never got to play with the great Brian Bevan. We overlapped slightly as he had a trial after I had returned to Germany following my first couple of appearances, but he then had to go to Australia for demobilisation and our paths never quite crossed. Harry Bath was another great player to join Warrington just after my time there.

Sadly Gerry and I also never played together again, although we became firm friends. He lived in Leigh and we started meeting socially and for extra fitness training sessions. Unfortunately he got the better of me when we met in the 1950 Challenge Cup final, winning the Lance Todd Trophy as Warrington beat Widnes in one of the biggest disappointments of my career. But there were no hard feelings and we later worked together at Leigh when I was on the board and he became coach.

*

Chapter Ten

The second incarnation of Leigh Rugby League Club began life without a home. The old ground at Mather Lane was sold by the owners, George Shaw's brewery, to the neighbours, Callender's cable works, in 1940. The buyers, who became British Insulated Callender's Cables (BICC) and the biggest manufacturer of electrical cables in the world soon after, were thriving and wanted to expand their Leigh plant. They needed the land for their own purposes and, unlike the brewery, had no interest in leasing it back to the rugby club.

That left Leigh as nomads but as the club and the sport ground to a halt due to the escalation of war soon after, the matter was all but forgotten. The club then lay dormant for so long that by 1945 it existed in name only. Fortunately, that is when James Hilton came in and set about rebuilding it with gusto.

I don't know what motivated Mr Hilton to get involved

but he was just the man Leigh needed. He was a successful local businessman who had done very well during the War. His principal business was in making washing machines and fridges for Littlewoods and I think he also produced boilers as well. He took over the mill where I used to work and converted it into a factory. It proved very lucrative for him but he also earned a handsome profit from producing munitions and other war materials.

Leigh RLFC was re-formed under James Hilton's supervision in late 1945, financed with £5,000 raised from the issue and sale of 10,000 new shares, a £1,500 interest-free loan from the Rugby Football League and £1,000 from other fund-raising activities. The club then announced the retention of all players previously on the books, including myself, and then began the task of looking for a new ground with a view to starting playing the following season.

Mr Hilton and his board of directors wanted the club to find a permanent home of its own but acquiring land and building on it was a long process, so a temporary facility had to be found to enable a team to fulfil fixtures in 1946-47. A deal was struck with the athletics club for the short-term use of their ground between Holden Road and Charles Street, which also happened to be adjacent to Mr Hilton's factory.

By the time that was secured, the process of building a new team was already well under way. Initially, the prospects looked bleak as only a mere handful of us had returned from the War and the reasons why the others had not were very sobering. Yet Mr Hilton's passion for the project was infectious and around those of us that had come back he had the nucleus of a promising new side. As well as myself, Ces Ryan, Peter Riley, Bob Montford, Percy Aldred and Albert Ord were all keen to play on and Mr Hilton rekindled our enthusiasm for playing for Leigh.

Among his new recruits was a promising half-back from

amateur side Culcheth called Frank Stirrup, whilst a few more gems were unearthed after adverts for trials attracted more than 100 hopefuls. Emlyn Jenkins, a brilliant stand-off for Salford and Great Britain in his day, was brought in as coach and momentum gathered. I attended the trials at Flapper Fold in Atherton myself and played well enough to be asked to captain the team. I was honoured. I had supported the club all my life and I was happy just to be able to represent them. Becoming their first post-war skipper was something else entirely and it made me immensely proud.

Our first outings after re-formation came in a couple of seven-a-side competitions in the summer of 1946 and the early signs were encouraging. We put up a spirited showing before being beaten by Salford in the first of those events at St Helens and then gave another good account of ourselves in front of 20,000 spectators at Central Park. The games may have lacked the intensity of regular rugby but the most important thing was that we were back on a field wearing Leigh jerseys. They were landmark occasions for the club and I for one, in my first run-out as captain, needed little motivation.

One other thing I remember from the Wigan tournament was how I made a fool of myself trying to kick a penalty. I always knew that when it came to goalkicking I had two left feet and I had not forgotten how silly I looked when my attempts at bisecting the uprights during an Army match ended in disaster. As far as I was concerned it was a task best left to others. Unfortunately not everyone shared my belief and it took another public demonstration to convince them.

After beating the Langworthy Juniors side in the preliminary round, we came up against Wigan in the first round proper and were given an excellent opportunity to take the lead when we were awarded a penalty in front of the posts. After the decision was made I picked up the ball and looked around expecting to see someone coming forward to kick the goal, but there was no movement. For some reason no-one was interested. I asked who was going to take it and everyone either looked away or shook their head. Much to my dismay, as captain, I realised I was going to have to take responsibility. At least it was straight, so it couldn't be that difficult – or so I thought.

Remarkably, I managed to mess it up completely. I really hadn't got a clue what I was doing and as I ran in I stubbed my toe in the ground and lost my footing as I swung for the ball. It ended up bobbling about five yards. My effort was even worse than my attempt to kick-off in the opening fixture at the new Leigh Sports Village in December 2008, and I was 90 years old by then!

That aside, the sevens tournaments served their purpose and we were back up and running. We flew into the new season with vigour and made an excellent start to the campaign. We won nine of our first 11 matches and pulled crowds of up to 10,000 to Charles Street. It was quite remarkable and an excellent reward for all James Hilton's efforts. Against the odds, Mr Hilton had put together what was arguably one of Leigh's best-ever sides and for a long time we actually looked capable of challenging for the title. In those days it was still logistically difficult to play every side twice and so the Championship was decided by a play-off series for the top four. We were in one of those positions for most of the season, only to hit a brick wall in the closing months and lose eight of our last nine.

Our first couple of games that season were away from home. We won on a waterlogged pitch at Rochdale on the opening day and I missed out on a try when I slipped in the mud going for the line. I was also stopped just short in the next game, at St Helens in the Lancashire Cup, but I made up for that when rugby league finally made its grand return to Leigh for the second leg of that tie a week later. We won 17-4 to complete a convincing aggregate success and I grabbed one of our three tries when I kicked through and beat Joe Ball and Frank Balmer in a race to the line. I could have had a couple more too but was called back by the referee on one break and was denied again when I was tackled just short. Yet it was the occasion that was the most important thing and the fact Leigh were once again playing in front of a home crowd. The ground was bursting at the seams and people had to be turned away before kick-off. The official attendance was given as 9,300 but the actual figure must have been closer to 10,000 because part of a hoarding on Holden Road gave way and many more got in without paying.

I was pleased with my form throughout the campaign, particularly during the first half of it when I played at centre. I scored again in a dour contest against Salford in early November, taking a long pass from Jack Simpson to help secure a morale-boosting first win over the Reds for 16 years. I followed that up with a match-winning try against Oldham in one of my best performances in a Leigh jersey. My try gave us our only points in a 3-2 home win and came when I dived on a kick from Stirrup after 30 minutes. I ran at the Oldham defence throughout the game and was only denied another after running onto a long kick from Jack Cayzer by a good tackle from Norman Harris.

It was the middle of November before we suffered our first league defeat, losing a close game at Warrington in which the great Brian Bevan made the difference. At home we were unbeaten until a Gus Risman-inspired Workington visited us in January. Risman, one of the legends of the game, was in the twilight of his career by then but was still a handful in his role as player/manager. We also lost a few other games to teams we should have beaten as our early-season form tailed off and we ended up finishing ninth. After the start we had that was disappointing but, considering our circumstances at the start of the season, it was pretty pleasing. I accept Leigh's difficult position after the War was by no means unique, as all clubs had plenty of problems to overcome, but to put together what we did from scratch was a very good effort. We enjoyed a couple of notable wins against Warrington and Widnes and with greater consistency in the second half of the campaign we could have finished higher. We went down at Bramley in one of only five games the bottom side won all season and lost twice in two ludicrous games against another struggling outfit in Featherstone.

The first of those was a total farce and should never have been played. The pitch at Post Office Road, already waterlogged after heavy rain, froze overnight and looked more like an ice rink than a rugby field. It was nothing short of dangerous and we were scared of going into tackles because if you hit your head it really hurt. Featherstone had actually tried to call the game off in the morning but couldn't get hold of anyone at Leigh because we had already set off. To make matters worse our train was delayed and we arrived with barely enough time to get changed. We went straight out onto the field to play and not surprisingly we lost. We didn't adapt to the conditions as well as they did and their freak winning try just about summed up the fiasco. The score was still 0-0 with just a few minutes remaining when two of our players lost possession in a desperate scramble and the ball bobbled loose for one of their players to dive on. A scoreless draw would have just been about fair from a game that tested everyone's tempers as balls bounced at jaunty angles on the rock-hard surface, no-one wanted to tackle and kicking prevailed. Things did boil over on a couple of occasions and one Featherstone player was knocked out cold by a stray boot. The one chance I had in the game came and went as I slid straight past the ball unable to stop. It is scarcely imaginable now, in these days of summer rugby, that a game could have been played in such treacherous conditions.

In total I made 33 out of a possible 42 appearances that season – a figure that would have been higher but for a handful of minor injuries – and scored six tries. One of those tries came in a tight win at Swinton after I had set up an earlier score for Teddy Kerwick by kicking ahead, regathering and passing to him out wide. I repeated that trick for my own try, following up my own kick and diving over.

I never considered myself an out-and-out try-scorer, although as a utility back I played on the wing a lot. I was more a creator of tries and preferred to play in the centre. I didn't feel I was at my best out wide. It was, of course, still very pleasing to score and I claimed one from a winger's position in front of a recorded 9,300 Charles Street crowd against Batley on New Year's Day 1947.

Throughout my time at Leigh I was used in a variety of positions. Stand-off was another I occupied regularly. I played the majority of my games at centre and would have preferred the stability of a permanent place there, but generally I was happy to play wherever I was selected. The only real exception came in a friendly against Barrow in summer 1947 when we unsuccessfully experimented with me at loose forward. That game was in Cornwall, of all places, after the Rugby Football League invited us to take part in an exhibition match as a reward for our successful post-war re-establishment. That was a nice honour for the Leigh club and a nice place to visit, but I didn't enjoy the game much. I was like a fish out of water.

Back at Charles Street, that new year crowd was one of

many good attendances we enjoyed that season. It really was a thrill to play in front of such healthy gates. Quite how we ever got so many in is still a mystery, though, because the facilities were terrible. The railings were also unnervingly close to the touchline and many times you ended up toppling over them and falling into the crowd. You needed them to help you get back up.

There was one occasion when the crowd got out of hand though – in our return match against Featherstone. It was Easter Monday and, backed by 10,000, we were keen to put on a show to make amends for the icy debacle of just a few weeks earlier. Unfortunately we actually produced one of our worst performances of the season to lose 7-4. It was a scrappy affair in which neither side scored a try and tempers often frayed, again. Both sides had a man sent off and my frustration was summed up when I knocked on having been presented with a good chance. But it was not only the players that performed poorly. The referee, a Mr F Seed, had an absolute shocker. He struggled to clamp down on niggly problems at the scrum and his decisions riled our supporters to such an extent that they went after him at the end of the game. Hundreds of angry fans swarmed around the dressing room and the official eventually had to leave the ground in a police car.

James Hilton said of the incident: "I have never seen such an example of disgraceful refereeing and if the problem is not tackled by the Rugby Football League then the standard of the game will never go any higher. Our supporters have never shown themselves to be anything but scrupulously fair, but the gross inefficiency shown today was enough to rouse the feelings of any enthusiastic follower of the game." All in all, I think we were quite glad to see the back of Featherstone for the season after that.

A couple of weeks after that I scored another very

pleasing try against Wigan, the outstanding side of the day, on what seemed a rare, for that season at least, sunny afternoon at Central Park. It came as we pieced together a good move from a scrum and I raced onto a Peter Riley kick to dive over. That got us back into the game after Wigan had scored the first two tries but the hosts then grabbed another and Teddy Kerwick's reply came too late as we lost 13-8 in front of a packed 27,000 crowd.

That game was one of a number of close contests we had with Wigan. Those derbies were always the games I looked forward to most, even though they were usually the hardest. Wigan had some great players at that time. The likes of Tommy Bradshaw, Ernie Ashcroft, Jack Cunliffe, Jack Hilton, Joe Egan and Ken Gee were all outstanding in that era and in one game I counted Wigan lining up against us with nine Great Britain internationals in their side. Yet we always gave a good account of ourselves and I don't remember them ever thrashing us. It was usually a great tussle and a close call. The intensity of the games was something else, and invariably there would be a big crowd stoking up the atmosphere.

Something else I loved about the Wigan clashes was the familiarity of the teams. The players knew each other so well we were on nickname terms – I was always 'Saley' – and that never ceased to add extra spice to the competition. Somehow the stakes just seemed higher when you were playing against mates and that made for some memorable encounters. I remember another game against them when I sidestepped about three players to score and Bradshaw, their cheeky but brilliant scrum-half, admitted I'd done him again afterwards. Bradshaw was a real character and, like many a great number seven, had a streak of impudence about him. He was always trying to demoralise us by chipping in with little comments here and there. He once tried to wind me up – and boast about his own virility – by telling me he had children that could run rings around me. It was clashes with players like him that made the derbies such great occasions.

Games against our other local rivals, namely St Helens, Warrington and Widnes, were always special too and it is a pity these sides aren't always in the same division these days. I think that's taken a bit out of the game. Swinton were another team that used to give us a lot of trouble back then and, east of the Pennines, Leeds and Bradford always provided a stern test.

Wigan proved the standout side of 1947 and my try at Central Park didn't worry them for too long as they went on to win the Championship for a second successive year a couple of months later. It was a pity we could not sustain our early season form but we were perhaps just a little lightweight in certain areas. The scrum proved a recurring problem and we tried five different players in the vital hooking role in search of the right formula. Scrums were fiercely contested in those days and a good hooker was worth his weight in gold. Even if he could barely run you'd happily carry him from one scrum to the next if you knew he was likely to win the ball. These days anyone can be a hooker because the ball never goes anywhere near them in the scrum. In fact, it often doesn't even go to the second row, just straight to the loose forward. It's ridiculous and they might as well not put the ball in at all. They have taken some of the skill out of the game and it's a shame. The scrums used to be such an important facet of any match and the contest they provided for the forwards added something that is missing now. People say rugby league is much faster and more attractive for having uncontested scrums but I miss the extra dimension they provided, even if they might have cost us a play-off chance in 1947.

Despite that, by the end of May we could still reflect on

a promising first season back in competition. It would have been nice to finish higher but considering what we had to play on, it was no mean feat. There are no two ways about it, Charles Street was the worst ground I ever played rugby on. It was absolutely diabolical because it was always muddy. There was a brook running next to the field and every time that flooded, so did the pitch. The drainage was very poor and the mud was usually ankle deep. It was nothing but a quagmire and you just had to plod through it. The other teams used to complain and ask how on earth we managed to play on it every other week. We actually wished we didn't have to. I suppose in the end we did get used to it, to a degree, and we probably did gain some sort of home advantage, but pretty rugby it was not.

By December of that season, after a spell of bad weather, the surface was nothing but mud and water. Conditions around the rest of the ground also got so bad that prior to a visit from St Helens it was decided that a section needed to be closed off for safety reasons and capacity reduced. Unfortunately rumour spread that the game itself had actually been called off and, in an attempt to raise a crowd, the club sent a loudspeaker van around the streets to advertise it.

As January came around things had got so bad that the club were embarrassed at the prospect of having to host holders Wakefield in the Challenge Cup. Given my horticultural background at Pennington Hall, I was asked to take a look at the drainage. With a team of workers I dug deep down but it was a hopeless task. The ground was beyond salvation. We ended up using a flame thrower to try to dry things out and dumped 300 tons of sand on the surface in an attempt to get the game on. As it happened the tie had to be postponed because of severe weather over the Pennines but our efforts were not in vain because the club rearranged a league game against Barrow at short notice for the same day. The use of so much sand also limited the impact of frost and, remarkably, we were one of the few grounds to get regular games on during the winter's cold snap. Such short-term measures were hardly ideal, however. It was like playing on Blackpool beach and we knew we would not be able to get away with it for long.

Thankfully we only had to play at Charles Street for one season before our new ground was ready. It was hardly going to be difficult to improve on the athletics ground but the difference after leaving there for Kirkhall Lane, or Hilton Park as it later and famously became known, was vast. Conditions were much improved and playing in ankle-deep mud became a thing of the past. After being put in charge of the building of the ground, I was at least going to make sure of that.

*

Chapter Eleven

As the team were toiling away at Charles Street, James Hilton was busy behind the scenes plotting the club's long-term future. He oversaw the purchase of five acres of land on Kirkhall Lane for £2,500 to pursue his dream of building a new permanent home for the club. That this came to fruition in time for the start of the 1947-48 season was testament not only to the determination of everyone at Leigh Rugby Football League Club but the togetherness and spirit of the whole community.

Leigh had already played at three different grounds when the search for a place to build a new one began. The club's first season in 1878-79 was played at Buck's Farm in Pennington but such was their popularity they moved to the Three Crowns field at Bedford after just one year. Ten years of steady progress then followed and by the time they moved on again to Frog Hall Field on Mather Lane in 1889, they were rated as one of the most powerful clubs in Lancashire.

These were the days before rugby league had split from rugby union and so the game was strictly amateur. As Leigh's profile grew, in common with a number of clubs in working-class areas, they wanted to start compensating players who had to take time off work on their behalf for loss of earnings. This was forbidden but Leigh incurred the wrath of the powers that be anyway when in 1893 they were found to have paid the removal expenses of a player from Wigan, Alfred Wallwork, who had joined them after moving to the town to work. As far as the lawmakers were concerned, this amounted to paying a professional and consequently Leigh became the first club to be suspended for breaking the game's amateur code. Wigan and Salford were suspended for similar offences soon after.

These suspensions were merely the tip of the iceberg as a number of clubs felt a responsibility to start paying players. By not doing so they feared they might not be able to sustain competitive teams. Yet the richer clubs down south and the Rugby Football Union top brass were horrified at such a prospect and the matter, of course, came to a head with the great split of 1895. Twenty-two clubs broke away to form the Northern Rugby Football Union and establish their own competition. The game of rugby league as we know it developed from there.

Leigh played through thick and thin at Mather Lane until the War, when the cable works took over the land. Charles Street then briefly became home number four in 1946 before the new ground at Kirkhall Lane opened its doors a year later.

My involvement in the building of Hilton Park, as the ground will always be remembered, is one of my proudest achievements. I worked many long, back-breaking hours on it as we raced against time to get it ready for action. I was at it virtually round the clock and I think my wife must have forgotten who I was, I spent that much time there. I rarely enjoyed a proper mealtime and had few really good nights' sleep. It wore me out in the end, and actually put me out of the game for a while, but the feeling of satisfaction when the ground opened was fantastic.

As I worked in the parks department the club asked for my help because they decided, in order to meet their own self-imposed deadline and avoid a second season at Charles Street, they would have to press ahead with their own labour. After acquiring the land, the task of levelling off a surface and laying turf had initially been put out to tender but no suitable parties were forthcoming. I was invited to oversee the operation and gladly accepted after the club reached an agreement with Leigh Corporation that essentially meant I could be seconded to the project for its duration. I threw my heart and soul into it and, with my team of enthusiastic volunteers from across the town, we turned a field of allotments in December 1946 into an operational rugby ground by the following August.

I was determined to produce a top-class pitch and one of my priorities, after the regular flooding farce at Charles Street, was to ensure it drained well. After knocking down a number of greenhouses and clearing the land, we dug down underneath where the pitch was to be and carefully laid a network of pipes. The drainage system we chose was known as the herringbone. It basically consisted of three six-inch pipes running parallel down the length of the field, one in the centre and one at either side. Interconnecting smaller pipes then ran diagonally, every five or six yards, from the middle pipe to the side drains. It was a system that proved very effective and Hilton Park seldom flooded throughout its history. Anyone who remembers a famous televised Challenge Cup tie against Salford in 2001 may beg to differ, but the only problem was that the pipes had not been flushed out in years. For most of the club's time there, the surface was very good.

After installing the drains we then had to lay the turf, which was a big operation and took some co-ordinating. Firstly we needed to collect the turf itself from where it was grown in Hale, Cheshire. For this we were very grateful for the help of local haulage businessman John Sumner, who had three big wagons to transport bales of cotton wool from the docks in Liverpool to the mills in Leigh. He gave us the use of these vehicles at the end of each day and would send them down to a garage in College Street we used as a meeting point. Our volunteers would then turn up after work, grab a quick cup of tea and a sandwich and then hop on to one of the trucks. There would be about five or six men per vehicle and they would drive over to Hale to dig up turf and bring it back.

They would tend to arrive back by about 7.30 or 8pm and by then we would have many pairs of hands ready to help lay it. I had a team of about 10 under my supervision during the day but this could swell to hundreds by the evening as we were flooded by well-wishers willing to offer assistance. Some nights you could hardly move because of the number of people. It really was incredible. The enthusiasm of the people of Leigh for the club and the new ground was absolutely fantastic and the camaraderie on the site each evening was brilliant. From then on I always said the ground really belonged to the Leigh public, not just the club, because it was they who built it.

When the turf arrived we would form a line and have people of all ages; children, parents and grandparents, all passing pieces along from the wagons to the pitch. I had the privilege of laying the first piece in the top corner at the railway end and we auctioned off the right to put down the last 10 bits to raise money. The father of club director Jack

Harding made the highest bid, £10, for the final piece and, to my astonishment, made the wonderful gesture of saying that if anyone deserved to put down the last sod, it was me. I was honoured and a photoshoot was arranged as I laid the piece in the bottom corner at the Glebe Street end.

Both those first and last pieces are now quietly growing in my garden after the groundsman dug them up when Hilton Park closed in 2008. It was a nice surprise when they made a presentation after the last game, although I had sensed something was going on when I was asked beforehand if I was going to be there. Given that I never missed games, it seemed a strange and unnecessary question. Of course I was going to be there! I soon realised why they'd asked, though, as they presented me with the turf. It was a lovely gesture from the club because it is not something that would ever have occurred to me. I had them planted in my lawn and I think my son Ronnie is now eying them up as part of his inheritance!

One thing we never found when the ground was dug up was the "lucky" silver horseshoe I was given by an old woman to place under the last piece of turf. It was nowhere to be found and I suspect it must have been disturbed years earlier when the floodlights were installed and part of the pitch took a battering. Mind you, given some of the bad luck Leigh had down the years, I had often been tempted to dig it up and throw it away anyway.

We were fortunate in many ways that the summer of 1947 was such a good one as it encouraged so many people to get outdoors and help. Yet such hot and dry weather had its drawbacks because it used to shrink the turf. The pitch needed regular watering but after a few all-nighters spraying it I struck on a novel way to do it. I went down to the fire station one day and asked if their men needed to practise. Their response was superb and every evening some firemen would turn up at 10pm to hose the grass. Sometimes they too would stay all night. They kept the pitch nice and green and prevented it shrinking. It was in great condition by the time of the first match.

I had little input in the building of the rest of the ground but that too took shape around us with the great support of the community. The Main Stand was actually transported and rebuilt brick by brick from Mather Lane, where it had first been erected in 1895. The cable works got in contact to say they had no use for it and were willing to give it away if we could remove it. A local builder called Bob Shaw, who was involved in the club at the time, took on the challenge and did a fine job. His achievement in rebuilding what became known as the Hilton Stand was all the more remarkable considering building materials were still in such short supply following the War.

The shale for the banking at the sides of the ground all came from Parsonage pit. A lot of it was being tipped along Wigan Road at the time so we asked if we could have some to create terraces for supporters. We finished them off at first with railway sleepers – I'm not sure where they came from! – before concreting them over a few years later. Some of the fencing around the outside of the ground came from old air raid shelters although they were later replaced by brick and wood. Again, a lot of this work was done by voluntary labour.

The support for the club at the time was out of this world and it is small wonder we averaged crowds of 10-12,000 when the ground opened. We actually got 17,000 for the first match, a Lancashire Cup tie against St Helens on August 30, 1947. The supporters' club had a committee of about 40 with another 40 waiting to get on. If anyone missed three meetings they were kicked off and someone else elected.

The grand opening of the ground was a great day. I'll

never forget it. I was again given the honour of captaining the side and played on the wing. We were beaten 15-0 by Saints, which took some of the gloss off the occasion, but it was still one of the greatest days in the club's history. The ground had been built in "almost a record space of time", as James Hilton said in his programme notes, and the future seemed so bright. The club's bold claims that the stadium could become the second best in rugby league behind only Wembley did not seem so fanciful at the time and there was no doubting it was the start of an exciting new era.

The commitment of Mr Hilton knew no bounds and it was a great honour for the club when he was elected chairman of the rugby league management committee in 1951. Everyone was shocked and saddened by his death in 1959. I think he was only 48 and it was a fitting tribute that the ground was subsequently renamed in his honour.

Because I experienced at first hand the work James Hilton put in, it annoyed me when in 2003 the club decided to rebrand Hilton Park as The Coliseum. By then, of course, the club were known as the Centurions and I could understand the logic, but to me it was just a marketing gimmick. James Hilton put so much money into the club and did more for it than any other chairman. Were it not for him Leigh might not even have restarted after the War. I never liked the Centurions moniker but I could at least live with that. I felt The Coliseum was a step too far and I tried to put my foot down. It did no good but I am pleased the club reverted to the old Hilton Park name before the ground closed down.

I have many happy memories of Hilton Park and I miss the friendliness and charm of the place. Leigh Sports Village is far better equipped but the character is completely different. The new stadium is run by a separate management company and they call all the shots. We must now abide by their rules and regulations and that has come as quite a culture shock after years of owning our own stadium. I know that times change and I'm pleased the club now has a state-of-the-art arena that can be of great benefit in the future, but that will not stop me missing Hilton Park.

I left Leigh for Widnes in 1949 but carried on living in the town and saw the ground continue to develop. The Supporters' Club Stand, built opposite the Hilton Stand, opened in 1950 and even though it was renamed the Tommy Sale Stand some five decades later, I have to admit it proved a bit of a white elephant. It was well built but poorly designed. When the builders put the first girder in, an old man stood watching them at the top of the banking went over and told them they had got their angles wrong. He said the angle needed to be much steeper or the stand would not offer great viewing. The builders took no notice and sent the old man on his way but that soon proved a mistake. When they came to put the seats in the upper tier it became apparent that you could hardly see the pitch if you were five rows back. The first 10 or 15 yards inside the touchline were completely out of sight. Nobody wanted to pay to sit there and people just ended up standing behind the seats.

After retiring as a player I soon got involved with Leigh again, firstly in a role with the supporters' club. As with the new stand, the supporters' club provided the bulk of the funds for the building of the ground's iconic scoreboard in 1959. Over the years fans grew attached to that scoreboard, which was reclad and repainted many times, and a campaign was set up to get it moved to the LSV. Sadly that was not to be. It was a big old thing and there was no room for it in the modern design, but the matter became irrelevant anyway because vandals set fire to it after the ground closed. That wasn't the only thing they did either. All the copper piping was stolen and various things were smashed.

It was sad to see Hilton Park in the state it was before it

was finally bulldozed in 2009. After all, it had been a major part of my life for its entire 61-year existence. I'll remember all the great games and players I watched there, the board meetings, functions, people and life in the office. And of course I played in plenty of games there I can never forget either, even if they did not all go according to plan. One in particular will haunt me forever, and more of that later, but even before then I had to regain my place in the team. Captaining the side on that first afternoon against St Helens was a joyous occasion and one that filled me with immense pride but little did I anticipate the fall that was to follow.

*

Chapter Twelve

After the euphoria of Kirkhall Lane's opening had subsided, the first two or three months there were actually quite upsetting for me. I didn't realise it at first but I'd worked myself out. After spending 15 or 16 hours at the ground most days for months I was badly in need of a break. I'd been starting first thing in the morning and not returning home until gone 10pm. That took its toll and as my training had been completely disrupted I was unable to perform at the required level when the rugby came round again.

It was obvious to me in the first few games of the season that I was not quite right. My legs had gone. I had no energy left and that did not go unnoticed by people at the club. I actually started the season reasonably well, getting involved in the making of two tries in a 16-5 win at Swinton on August 23, but it was a struggle. I was then below par in our historic home match with St Helens and after we were thrashed in the second leg of that Lancashire Cup tie a few days later, I was told I should rest for a month.

I was dropped for the next game against Rochdale but actually earned a last-minute reprieve due to injuries. I didn't play particularly well and although I ended up playing in the next couple of matches as well, the club were still adamant that I needed to take time out. They felt it was essential that I took a complete break before concentrating on training for a while and then playing again. It was good advice but I was still reluctant to do it. I didn't want to miss any rugby and I found being dropped hard to take. I was also disappointed to see the captaincy handed over to Teddy Kerwick. I had nothing against him personally but it was frustrating to lose something I cherished so proudly.

Yet deep down I knew there could be no room for sentiment and I took what I was told on board. I did as I was asked and rested and it did me a power of good. When I returned I realised just how off the pace I had been. Fully refreshed, I was like a different player from how I was before the break. I was then able to play a full part in what proved a reasonable season for Leigh. We finished 14th with 18 wins from 36 games and I made 26 appearances in all competitions, scoring six tries.

I actually saw little action until Christmas, although I was briefly recalled for a match against the New Zealand tourists in mid-October. We were narrowly beaten 10-5 in front of 15,847 at Kirkhall Lane and, due to injuries, I kept my place to play Hull a few days later. After that, however, I had to wait until our trip to St Helens on Christmas Day for another chance. We were hammered 22-3 but at least I took my opportunity by scoring our try and I was retained for the subsequent games on Boxing Day, December 27, New Year's Day and January 3. That was quite a programme but nothing particularly unusual back then. We'd often get fixtures in blocks such as that and just had to get on with it. We'd try to run any bruises off. I'll admit my wife did help me into bed a lot, though. Sometimes I was just so sore it was a real struggle on my own. I didn't think much of it back then but when I watch games now and I see tackles that seem far harder than any in my day, I know modern players must really feel it after they've played.

The win over Saints on New Year's Day was when I knew I was really back in business. It was muddy underfoot but I relished the conditions and made a try for Eric Parr by collecting my own kick and then putting him clear. I was also denied a try myself by a good tackle and I did plenty of defensive work as we held on for an 8-3 triumph.

I was switched to half-back soon after that and scored in another muddy win, this time against Salford, by kicking a loose ball forward and diving over the line. I touched down again in a defeat at Halifax in the snow, taking a Frank Daley pass and weaving my way through, and by the end of January I was playing on the wing.

It was a really exciting time to be involved at Leigh. Crowds flocked to the new ground and the feelgood factor was cranked up a notch midway through the season when the club splashed out a world record fee for Dewsbury's goalkicking full-back Jimmy Ledgard. What a brilliant signing that was. Jimmy already had quite a reputation and his arrival in January 1948 for a then hefty £2,650 got the town buzzing. It was another clear statement of James Hilton's ambition and Jimmy was not only an immediate hit but went on to become a Leigh legend.

He was an absolute joy to play alongside. As I have mentioned elsewhere, he was an outstanding kicker. He could make the ball swerve one way or the other and land it exactly where he wanted. His ability to find touch was unrivalled and he rewrote the club's record books in terms of goals. Yet there was far more to his game than just kicking as he could catch a ball thrown at him at almost any speed and from the most awkward of angles. However you threw it at him he would somehow take it. He was a wonder to behold and it was very reassuring to have such a player in the side. We were all very excited when we heard he was coming to Leigh.

Jimmy added to what was already a useful side. One player from that era I shall certainly never forget was the forward Charlie Pawsey. He was a real hard case who could give it and take it, but he certainly dished out more than he received. For most of the time I was glad to be on the same side but I did have to play against him once, after I'd moved on to Widnes. By that time Leigh had also signed another fearsome forward who went on to serve the club with distinction in Stan Owen, so I endured a bruising afternoon. At one point I tackled Charlie from behind and ended up pulling him back on top of me. As we went down he thrust his head back into my face in frustration and connected with my nose at full force. It didn't half hurt! At the time he claimed he didn't know it was me, but I didn't believe him. There was no love lost between friends when meeting in opposition.

Of the rest, Ted Kerwick was a bit of a loner off the field but he was an excellent three-quarter and we also had a very good scrum-half in Peter Riley. Frank Daley was a decent centre and he combined well with Percy Aldred on the right wing. Jimmy Pendlebury, our full-back when the team reformed, was only a small fella but a good player. Alan Ackers was another fine full-back but his chances became limited after Ledgard arrived.

I forced my way over for another try in a home win over Swinton while the other two I scored that season came in games against Barrow. For some reason I often scored against them, even though I never enjoyed travelling up there. That was a real drag. It used to take so long to travel to Barrow or the other Cumberland grounds by coach that we would have to stop and have a meal somewhere. Sometimes it was easier to take the train, if there was one running, although at Barrow we'd have to walk over a field from the station on our arrival. We were usually guaranteed a tough game when we got there too and it was the same at Whitehaven and Workington. Reaching the Hull clubs was also pretty arduous in those days. The journey can be tough enough now, with all that traffic on the M62, but it was even more of a pain before that motorway so familiar to all in rugby league was built. It used to take five or six hours just to get there and if we could we'd get a train from Manchester. Despite all that, though, my least favourite away ground had to be Batley. The sloping pitch made Mount Pleasant a terrible place to play.

The area of the team where we were perhaps the most unsettled during the 1947-48 season was the coaching department due to a number of changes in a short space of time. Laurie Higgins began the year in charge after Emlyn Jenkins left for Warrington but he did not last long. Higgins had a good reputation as a player from his pre-War days at Halifax and he was committed to the town of Leigh with an established business, a tailor's shop, nearby. In later years he would become a director at the club but he did not prove a successful coach. He resigned in January 1948 and Jack "Cod" Miller, so called because his mother had a fish shop down Leigh Road, took over. Miller had made a few appearances for us during our season at Charles Street, bringing with him the toughness for which he had become renowned during his career at Warrington. Yet he too proved short-lived as a coach and at the end of the season Jenkins was brought back as player-coach/manager.

I did not enjoy the best of starts to the 1948-49 season as I was left out for the first couple of games and actually played just three of the opening nine, as a winger. It was the first indication that I was no longer first choice at centre. I thought I had turned it all around, however, when I returned to the side and claimed a try against the Australian tourists. That was a huge career highlight.

Playing against Australia for Great Britain was an ambition I never achieved because I was not good enough for international rugby. There were plenty of better centres around such as Ernest Ashcroft at Wigan and Bradford's Jack Kitching and so the possibility never arose. I couldn't even make the Lancashire side either, so facing the Kangaroos in a tour match at Leigh was the next best thing. I was very proud to get on the scoresheet that day and I remember it as if it were yesterday.

Throughout my career I was known as 'The Diver'. I always felt I could dive out of a tackle or if I got within five yards of the tryline I could cover the ground quicker by diving. I finished most of my tries by projecting myself over the line and another nickname I earned was Esther Williams, after the famous swimmer and diver-turned-Hollywood actress. The good old *Leigh Journal* also got in on the act as their cartoonist used my dives as a source for his material.

Normally whenever I got a sniff of the line I would dive and in one second-half raid on the Aussie line this instinct took over. I actually got my calculations slightly out as I landed an inch or two short but I pushed it over as momentum carried me forward and nobody was any the wiser. It wasn't enough to prevent us losing 24-12 but it was definitely a moment to savour on a night we did ourselves proud in front of 13,000 at Kirkhall Lane. We played most of the game with just 12 men after Desmond Clarkson went off injured with just 10 minutes gone but we battled away and gave the Australians a really good run for their money.

Sadly the elation did not last as I came crashing back to

earth in the most spectacular of fashions. There was initial disappointment as I played poorly in the next two games against Liverpool Stanley and Batley, despite being back in my favoured position at centre. At the time I was approaching the final stages of my teaching qualification but I didn't use that as an excuse. I was not at my best and, having kept my place in the team, I was frustrated not to have made the most of my opportunities. However, being irritated at a mere loss of form was nothing compared with what I went through after the visit of Halifax on October 16, 1948. Even now, I still shudder at the memory of that afternoon and the incredible blunder that marked the beginning of the end of my Leigh career. Players like to be remembered for the tries they scored. But it is for one I infamously didn't score on that day that my time as a Leigh player is best remembered.

It was a match we should have won and would have done had I not committed the rugby equivalent of missing an open goal from two yards. It happened with the game at a tense stage. We were defending deep inside our own half when an opportunity suddenly opened up for me to make myself a hero. I spotted a gap as I took a Jimmy Rowe pass and darted through it. I broke the line and confidence flooded through me as I quickly got into my stride. I decided to take the whole Halifax team on and pinned my ears back. I never ran as fast in my life as I did then as I homed in on their line, swerving around their desperate tackles on the way. I beat everyone and was about to celebrate a magnificent, match-winning try when disaster struck. Bravado got the better of me and I decided to dive over the line in typically flamboyant fashion. It was a horrendous mistake. As I leapt I somehow contrived to knock the ball out of my hands with my knee and it bounced away. The chance went with it and I just wanted the earth to swallow me whole. It was the most embarrassing moment of my life.

All I had to do was put the ball down but I messed it up and that moment has haunted me ever since.

The Halifax players couldn't believe their luck. They rushed to me in my humiliation to congratulate me. "Well done Saley, you've won us the match," they said. I cried without sound as they patted me on the back and rubbed it in. My team-mates tried to dig me out of my predicament as Frank Alder scored a fine late try to ensure we escaped with a 10-10 draw, and Percy Aldred then went close to snatching victory in the last minute, but my pain could not be eased.

Foolishly, I went out for a few drinks in town that night and just about everyone mentioned it. I got stick all night, and that was just the start. The local papers had their say a few days later and I then had even fewer places to hide. The *Leigh Journal* bemoaned how I, "in trying to execute a spectacular dive lost the ball and a certain try". The *Leigh Chronicle* referred to my moment of ignominy as a "wasted effort" and added: "When a yard from the line Sale made a spectacular dive over the line, but dropped the ball and so threw a splendid chance away."

The incident went down in local folklore and I heard of coaches teaching children to ground the ball properly and not "do a Tommy Sale". It still crops up now when people speak about me, as if that's all they know me for. "Saley, remember dropping that ball over the line?" they ask. Do I remember? Sixty-one years and I'm still being reminded of it! Whenever someone drops a ball over the line people say they've done Saley's trick! The decades since have eased the anguish but I've never fully escaped it. I still replay the incident in my mind, as I have done thousands of times over the years, and I just wish I could ground the ball safely.

Some 20 years after my faux pas I was at Wembley when Don Fox notoriously missed that last-minute conversion to win the Challenge Cup and I knew exactly how he felt. It was a horrible moment and I felt so sorry for him. He was a magnificent player but, in the years that followed, that kick almost invariably became what people remembered him for. It was something he never lived down. At least my moment of ignominy didn't come in front of 87,100 people at the national stadium, nor make many newsreels, but at the time it was bad enough. I have no doubt the writing was on the wall for my Leigh career from that moment.

Things certainly went downhill for me from then onwards. The rest of 1948-49 season was a huge letdown as I fell out of favour and the team struggled. I was not only dropped after my gaffe but was even overlooked for A team duties in the weeks that followed. I featured only fitfully thereafter and made just 11 appearances in total throughout the whole campaign. My try against Australia, the source of so much pleasure and optimism when I scored it, was the only time I crossed the whitewash and sadly proved my last before I was sold to Widnes midway through the following season.

The team itself won less than half its games and finished a disappointing 18th, although they had a right to feel a little aggrieved after a bizarre elimination from the Challenge Cup. In one of the most extraordinary episodes in the club's history, the lads produced a superb performance to beat holders Wigan 12-11 at Central Park in the first of two legs, but were then narrowly edged out 5-4 in the return. Under the rules, extra time should then have been played but the referee blundered and ordered a replay. Controversy ensued but ultimately all the Rugby Football League could do was annul the result of the second leg and insist that be replayed. That at least restored Leigh's slender first-leg advantage but they could not repeat their heroics for a third successive game and were beaten 10-4.

The club also had problems off the field as the directors

faced a vote of no confidence over their handling of certain affairs, but there were some positives from the season. Home crowds remained excellent throughout and a number of players continued to perform outstandingly. Ledgard kicked goals for fun and was selected for Great Britain, England and Yorkshire, while Norman Harris and Jack Bowen turned out for Wales. Rowe emerged as a good stand-off and was picked to play for Lancashire along with Kerwick, Riley and Ben Coffey. All that, of course, was of little consolation to me at the time. My days as a Leigh player seemed numbered and when I was frozen out at the start of the 1949-50 season I thought my career was over.

*

Chapter Thirteen

In 1949 my rugby career hit rock bottom. I was summoned to the boardroom by James Hilton and told, in as many words, that I was surplus to requirements and was being placed on the transfer list. They were making me available at a low fee of £450 in the hope it would attract some interest. Despite my lack of games I hadn't seen that coming and I went home absolutely shattered. I was devastated and cried when I got there.

In my time at Leigh I had always been one of the hardest trainers in the squad. I used to work on my fitness every night of the week. The club would train on Tuesdays and Thursdays but I supplemented that with extra sprint sessions on Mondays, Wednesdays and Fridays after work. My training partner was Warrington's Gerry Helme, with whom I had been firm friends ever since the day we had both been asked to sign for the Wire together after the War. Gerry was as keen on his fitness as I was and, although he played for Warrington, he never moved away from the

Leigh area. We used to meet at the athletics club at Charles Street and do a lot of work on the track with the sprinters. If I could be sure of one thing when I was on the field, it was that I was fit. You need to be in good shape to have a chance of succeeding and enjoying the game.

I maintained my training schedule throughout the 1948-49 season, even when I was struggling to win a place in the team. Yet the bombshell of being told that I was up for sale completely demoralised me. It knocked all the enthusiasm out of me and I began to wonder what the point of working so hard was. When the 1949-50 campaign began I found I was in the cold completely and was not even getting picked for the A team. As the weeks went by I realised it was a situation that was unlikely to change and I began to think my time in the professional game was over. The first team did well enough without me, reaching the Lancashire Cup final in October 1949, and if I wasn't getting into the A team it seemed I really didn't have much chance. I had always been so proud to play for Leigh, it had been my ambition since childhood, but I was very hurt by the way they had written me off.

But whatever they thought, I was not going to stop playing completely. I'd already lost six of my best years during the War and I didn't want to give up when I still felt, at 31, I could go on for two or three more. I wanted to carry on, even if it was at a lower level, so I joined the Wigan Road Working Men's Club and turned out for their amateur side. They played at the Marsh Playing Fields, which was incidentally part of a park I had helped build, and they were a pretty handy team. I was asked to captain them and things went so well on the field that one particularly good game caught the attention of a passing scout from Widnes.

That proved to be just the stroke of luck I needed. He approached me and asked me what on earth I was doing playing for an amateur team. He obviously knew who I was because he called me Saley. I explained that I was on the transfer list at Leigh and could no longer get into the side. He seemed genuinely surprised and said that I should still be playing because I had clearly not lost my touch. He said I should forget them and join Widnes.

I was flattered by the approach but initially reluctant, simply because I had always loved Leigh so much. I still didn't want to leave. I resisted the overtures at first but thankfully Widnes were persistent and persuasive. With a heavy heart, I came to the conclusion that I had no future at my hometown club and had nothing to lose by joining Widnes. It was a wrench at the time but I soon found the grass was greener elsewhere and I never regretted it. I signed for Widnes for a reported £425 on December 9, 1949 and it was the best thing that could have happened to me.

The transformation was remarkable and I went on to play the best rugby of my life in two superb years at Naughton Park. I was made to feel so welcome and it was such a great feeling to be wanted again that I was completely reinvigorated. I picked up all my old training routines and had an extra spring in my step. I went straight into the team and, fuelled by a newfound enthusiasm, I impressed enough to be made captain after playing just two games. That took my game up yet another level as I relished the responsibility. The season then became something of a fairytale story as we hit a rich vein of form that culminated with me leading the team out in front of 94,249 people at Wembley after we beat the odds to reach the Challenge Cup final. From where I had come from at the start of the season, that was an experience that was simply beyond my wildest dreams. Along the way I produced my greatest performance with a man-of-the-match display against the mighty Bradford Northern in the semi-finals. The elation I felt after that was unbelievable and took my career to a peak it would never have reached had I kicked my heels at Leigh.

Leigh was, and of course still is, my first love and people have always asked me why I left. To them my reply is simple. I never left Leigh, Leigh left me. I had some great times at my hometown club but they threw me on the scrapheap. In the end, I couldn't refuse the move. I left Leigh having made 82 appearances over 11 war-interrupted years, scored 16 tries and, remarkably, kicked those two goals.

*

Chapter Fourteen

I was a bit apprehensive when I first arrived at Widnes. I had never envisaged plying my trade away from Leigh before and the new surroundings made me feel a little nervous. I was also conscious of the fact that I was an outsider. At the time Widnes had a strong reputation for producing homegrown players and their squad was packed with local lads. The only other players from out of town were Jackie Fleming, who arrived a couple of months after I did, and another recent signing in Bob Band. Even though I was coming from just 20 miles down the road, I still wondered whether I would fit in.

As it turned out I needn't have worried. I was never treated any differently to anyone else and I settled very quickly. Widnes showed faith in me from the start and that gave me a new lease of life. It was so refreshing after effectively being told by Leigh that I was past it.

One of the things I especially enjoyed at Widnes was the

chance to play regularly in my preferred position of centre again. Towards the end of my time at Leigh I'd been shuffled around just a bit too much for my liking and having a settled position made such a difference. At first it seemed Widnes saw me as a stand-off but I was soon moved to centre and established myself as first choice. The team and the way they played also suited me perfectly and I was not only uplifted, but a player transformed. What followed were undoubtedly the best days of my career.

A centre's job is to play for his winger and I teamed up with a good wide man at Widnes in Gus Malone. I sent him flying down the touchline many times. He actually benefited from plenty of passes when I probably could have gone for the line myself, but I usually wanted to make it absolutely certain we scored. More often than not I could rely on him to finish off an attack.

That said, I was far more prolific at Widnes than I had been previously, simply because I was a lot more confident a player. The trust the club put in me from day one manifested itself immediately in more determined performances and I went for gaps or for the line much more often than I had in the past. At Leigh I had perhaps been too hesitant but with Widnes I played like I had nothing to lose. I had been given a second chance in the professional game and wanted to make the most of it.

My first season at Naughton Park could hardly have gone better. To go from the Marsh Playing Fields to Wembley in the space of a few months was out of this world. I couldn't believe how quickly things happened after I signed. Just a day later I was in the team and making my debut, despite snow and freezing conditions, in a home match against Huddersfield. The game ended in defeat, as did the first three after I joined, but by the time I tasted my first victory, against Whitehaven on Boxing Day, I had already been made captain.

Chapter Fourteen

League honours were already out of reach but momentum began to gather thereon and I scored my first two Chemics tries in a 42-7 thrashing of York in early January. We started to find some consistency and the start of the Challenge Cup competition, which was played in the second half of the season, came at just the right time.

I scored five tries in as many games in the cup as we embarked on a run that led us all the way to the final. Everything on the field just seemed to go right for me and my confidence grew with every win. I didn't make the scoresheet in our first outing in the competition, a 15-2 first-leg win over Rochdale capped by a fine try from Gus, but I made up for that in the return by touching down twice. It was a game played in abysmal weather, with sheets of hail and sleet falling throughout, and we had to work hard. The score was 0-0 at half-time but I eventually broke the deadlock five minutes after the restart by finishing a good move. After that we stepped up and eased to a 27-0 win. I claimed my second from an interception inside the Rochdale '25' and it was great to hear afterwards, via team-mate Fred Higgins, whose brother Alec was on the committee, that the watching top brass had almost started celebrating as soon as I had caught the ball, so confident were they that I would score.

We were given what some considered a kind draw against Batley in the second round but it proved anything but until Danny Naughton scored twice in the second half to see us through. Danny was an outstanding prop forward who not only tackled but scored and created tries too. He was a huge powerful player with great hands. He was tough enough to stop as it was, but it was even harder to prevent him passing. I benefitted from his good work many times and I remember one try in particular when he powered towards the line, guarding the ball closely, until he was halted just short. I knew he would still be able to keep the ball alive and I just gave a little call as I ran past. "Here Danny," I yelled, and he instinctively found me with a cute little pass that sent me under the posts. His value to the side was immense and he thoroughly deserved his Great Britain call-up that year. It was just a pity the ship for Australia set sail before the end of the season and we lost him for the cup final.

But that was only after we got through Barrow in the third round and a daunting semi-final date with cup kings Bradford. Pleasingly, I maintained my normal scoring service against Barrow by taking a pass from Jackie Fleming to go over. I then sent Gus away down the left wing for the try that clinched an exciting 12-7 win.

We played Barrow again a couple of weeks later in the league and I maintained my hot streak by grabbing another try as we warmed up for the semi-final with a 20-6 win. It was a run out we felt we needed as Bradford was just about the toughest possible assignment we could have been handed in our bid to reach Wembley. With each cup win I kept telling the lads we had a chance of getting there but when the semi-final draw was made we were immediately written off in most quarters. Bradford had won the cup the previous year and were bidding to reach a Wembley final for a record fourth consecutive year. Bradford were an outstanding team and everyone thought they were going to win – but I stopped them.

*

Chapter Fifteen

Saturday, April 1, 1950 was the date and Central Park, Wigan, the venue for the greatest game I ever played. Never will I forget the feeling of jubilation as I was carried off on the shoulders of my team-mates after scoring the two tries that took Widnes to Wembley. It was undoubtedly one of the proudest moments of my life.

Yet the game took some winning. Bradford were red-hot favourites and I heard some bookies were offering odds on us beating them of 40/1. We knew we could not afford to let them settle and had to get into them straightaway. I told the lads we really had to get stuck in and kept repeating the message throughout the game. That got them fully fired up and it paid off. We smothered Bradford every time they got the ball and that made for a really tight encounter. After a lot of hard work early on we got the break we needed before half-time as I claimed the first try in the bottom corner.

It came in typical fashion as I dived for the line after a good team move down the left but I freely admit I was a bit sneaky. I landed just short but I pushed the ball over and got away with it. It was only a matter of inches and very subtle but a few of the Bradford players saw what happened and surrounded the referee, Albert Dobson, in protest. These days a video ref would have disallowed it but thankfully he stuck by his decision. I was happy to take whatever luck came my way as there was a lot at stake and I didn't feel guilty about it. I was so determined to win that it was almost a case of doing it by fair means or foul. Besides, I felt I deserved the try for effort anyway.

With Colin Hutton missing the goal we only had a slender lead and needed to focus on our defence once again. I wouldn't leave our lads alone. I was shouting at them all the time, urging them to follow me and get in and tackle every time Bradford got the ball. I knew if we gave them any space they'd run rings around us and we couldn't slacken off. We had to get forward and stop them running. I think it is bad play for a team to stand back and let opponents come to them. The defensive line should always get forward to try to meet them. Allowing a team to run can spell danger, particularly close to the line as the big forwards can burst through. If big men are allowed to get into their stride they can take some stopping and we had to be wary of that.

Only once were we caught out as Jackie Fleming missed a tackle and his man got away. That exposed our full-back Frank Bradley and had he been sidestepped to the left I'm convinced Bradford would have scored. Fortunately, with only a split second to make his choice, the ball-carrier went right and I was able to catch him with a flying dive. As I lay on the deck relieved after hauling him down, Jackie came up to me and said he wouldn't do that again. "You'd better not!" I barked, or words to that effect.

Aside from that scare, our plan worked to perfection. Bradford were not used to such pressure and I stung them further with my second try 17 minutes into the second half. Play had stalled on the right but we broke away quickly and spread it to the left. Gus Malone, a true hero after being cut and concussed in an early tackle, then picked me out and I gleefully dived over in the corner. Colin Hutton, my great friend and fellow centre, then held his nerve to kick the goal, brilliantly, from the touchline. The wind had made kicking difficult for him all afternoon and he had been unfortunate with a couple of penalties, including one that hit the upright, but this time his effort curved beautifully between the sticks. I was more chuffed to see that than I was at scoring the try because I knew it had put us within touching distance. I still made sure we stayed focused on defence in the closing stages but time eventually ran out for Bradford and we started to celebrate a famous 8-0 win.

It had been my finest 80 minutes on a rugby field and the players rushed in to carry me off. In attack, defence and as a captain I don't think I could have played better. I was on cloud nine and I savoured every last moment of it. I have highlights of the game on video now and happy memories come flooding back whenever I watch it.

I couldn't believe who the first man to congratulate me when I got back to the changing rooms was; none other than James Hilton, the man who had put me on the transfer list at Leigh. I was shocked but pleased to see him.

"Congratulations Tommy," he said. "I'm very pleased for you."

He was absolutely genuine but I couldn't resist a go back.

"Congratulations?" I asked. "No, congratulations to you – for putting me on the transfer list!"

I told him he'd done me the best turn I've ever had in my life by selling me. Things had worked out unbelievably well and I was now on my way to Wembley.

He was a good chap, James Hilton. He put a lot of money into Leigh to get the club started again and I had great respect for him. However, I was deeply hurt the day he told me I was surplus to requirements. I was heartbroken but with my performance at Central Park that day I felt I'd got the last laugh. It was something that made victory all the sweeter.

Not surprisingly the Bradford lads were dejected in the bath afterwards. At Wigan all the players used to jump into one big communal bath and, looking back, it's amazing none of them clocked any of us. We were splashing around and full of ourselves while they sat there glum-faced. Talk about rubbing it in. They were absolutely gutted. Defeat was something they hadn't countenanced and they couldn't believe we'd outplayed them so comprehensively. To be honest, they had rarely even looked like scoring. As the game wore on I knew we were getting to them and it was just a case of holding our nerve. We never gave them a chance and I was especially proud of the number Colin and I did on our opposite numbers Jack Kitching and Ernest Ward, who at the time were Great Britain's first-choice centre pairing.

The celebrations continued long after getting out of the bath and the papers on Monday morning were a sight to behold. I particularly treasure one cutting with a picture of me diving head-on, arms outstretched, to score my second. Ken Traill, the Bradford loose forward, is groping at air in a vain attempt to stop me. The headline above it simply reads, "This try spelt Wembley". That picture later won sports photograph of the year and Widnes have a large version of it on the wall of their museum.

From that day on it was impossible not to think about the cup final. Over the next five weeks thoughts of Wembley and the Twin Towers filled our minds and our form suffered.

Chapter Fifteen

We played six games between the semi-final and final and won just two of them, both against Liverpool Stanley. I at least maintained my scoring touch by claiming another double in our first outing after the semi-final, a Wembley dress rehearsal against Warrington, as well as grabbing one in each of the Liverpool fixtures. Yet our three games immediately prior to the final were dismal affairs. We were nilled by Belle Vue and then managed a grand total of just four points in losing first to a Wigan team missing eight tourists and then to a 12-man Leigh side, Colin Hutton kicking a goal in each game.

Perhaps that was only to be expected. We were out of contention in the league and winning the cup was all that mattered. The fact local rivals Warrington were to be our opponents heightened the anticipation and it was impossible not to be distracted. The game completely captured the imagination of the whole area and there was no escaping it. It had been 13 years since Widnes had last claimed the cup, a period that seemed even longer because of the War, and Warrington had never won at Wembley. Everyone was talking about it and everyone wanted to be there.

We enjoyed the build-up. We were suddenly the focus of a lot of attention and we lapped it up. There was plenty of press coverage and lots of people wanting to meet us. One thing we got involved in was an advertising campaign for Philips. They had a new electric razor out at the time and we were used for a lot of publicity shots. We were all pictured shaving and each got a razor for our troubles. It wasn't bad either and I actually kept mine for quite a few years.

The final weekend as a whole was a wonderful experience. We all travelled down to London together on the train from Liverpool and the camaraderie was superb. Everyone was looking forward to the game so much.

Adding to the adventure was a tour of the Houses of Parliament organised by the newly-elected Widnes MP James MacColl. Things like that just made the occasion all the more memorable.

I'll also never forget the roar as we walked out onto the pitch in front of that 94,000-plus full house. It was something to savour, as was meeting Prime Minister Clement Atlee and introducing him to all the team. The game was also one of the few that Evelyne, my wife, came to watch me play. I managed to pick her out in the crowd and gave her a wave.

Sadly, the game itself was a bitter pill to swallow. At the end of the day there is no joy in going to Wembley and losing. The tables were well and truly turned on us as Warrington gave us a taste of what we had inflicted on Bradford in the previous round. Their gameplan was superb and they never gave us a chance. We just could not get the ball off them and they ran out deserved winners, 19-0.

Warrington's hooker, Ike Fishwick, was outstanding that day and made a huge difference. He kept winning the ball for them and all we were doing was chasing and tackling. We still gave it everything and with the amount of possession Warrington had they probably should have scored about 60 points, but we just couldn't get anything going. We barely saw their line and they were always on ours. Whenever we got near their half we'd have to kick downfield and they'd come away with the ball from the resulting scrum and be back on our line in no time. It was painful stuff.

Despite Fishwick's performance, it was my old friend Gerry Helme who won the Lance Todd Trophy as man of the match. He was brilliant. He ran the show and whenever we got in their half it was inevitable Gerry was going to get the ball and force us back. His kicking game was outstanding. He found touch so many times and we couldn't break the shackles. He was a good mate but I was cursing him throughout. I told him afterwards I'd wished his foot would drop off!

It certainly didn't help that we were denied the services of two of our best players in Danny Naughton and Fred Higgins. They'd been just a bit too good and earned selection for Great Britain. At the time of the match they were already on the slow boat to Australia with the rest of the tourists. That was unfortunate and made a big difference to our team because their pack swamped ours. Yet that should not be an excuse as Warrington were definitely a better side than we were and they too had a couple of tourists missing in Bob Ryan and Jim Featherstone. I just wished we could have got a bit more ball to give them a run for their money.

It was the biggest anti-climax of my career. I remember vividly walking back down the tunnel after the game and turning back to see Warrington doing a lap of honour with the cup. It was horrible and it broke my heart but at least I can say I got there. That is the main thing. When you go into this game you have two desires, one to play for your country and the other to play at Wembley. At least I achieved one of them. It was still a lovely weekend overall and the club really did us proud. Someone had to be the losers. I'm proud to have been involved and I'll always cherish my medal, as I'm sure did a lot of the other lads. I look back on our team photos with great pride and it's sad so few of them are still with us now. John Parkes, one of the youngest members of the side, was the first to pass away, dying tragically in his 30s. That was a devastating blow.

Before we left London on the Monday after the game, the fans that had travelled south lined up at Euston Station to give us a tumultuous send-off. Given the nature of the defeat that was astounding, but more was to follow as we were feted like heroes when we arrived back in Widnes. The people turned out in huge numbers to welcome us back and the market square was packed. It was as if we had won the cup. I was completely taken aback as I had not been expecting any kind of public reception at all. I didn't think there'd be anyone there. I was touched by the show of support but at the same time felt guilty for letting them down in such a disappointing manner. We were taken up onto the balcony at the town hall and I said sorry.

"Ladies and gentlemen will you please accept my apologies for the display we gave on Saturday," I said. Yet everyone was lovely. I found at Widnes they always were. I enjoyed every minute I spent at that club and whenever I go back now they always make a fuss of me. I really cannot speak highly enough of the place.

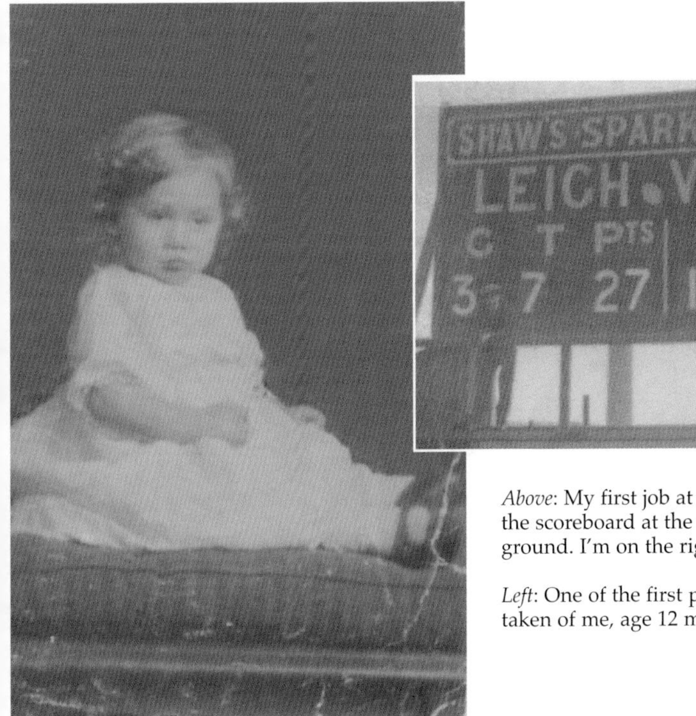

Above: My first job at Leigh, operating the scoreboard at the old Mather Lane ground. I'm on the right.

Left: One of the first pictures ever taken of me, age 12 months.

Below: My first team, the Leigh supporters' club junior side. I thought I was one of the worst players in the team but was actually the only one to make it professionally. That's me front right, sitting cross-legged.

LEIGH RUGBY SUPPORTERS CLUB
SEASON 1932 - 33

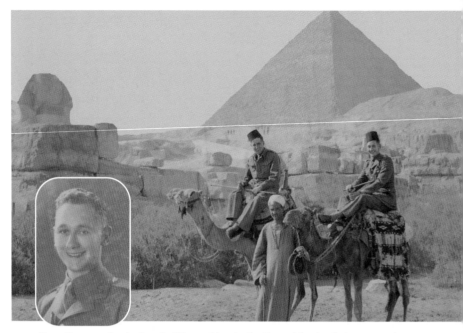

Above: Rare respite during the War - taking in the Pyramids after being granted leave in Egypt. *Inset*: A proud moment - being made a lieutenant after a gruelling six months at the Officer Cadet Training Unit in Palestine.

Above: Rhine Army v Kiwis at Wuppertal, Germany, March 1946. It was a great honour to play for the Forces against the touring New Zealanders, many of whom went on to become All Blacks. I'm on the second row, third right. Bert Cook, later of Leeds, is crouched down in front of me while St Helens legend Jimmy Stott is stood on the third row, far left.

Left: Playing against Wigan (Bob Shuttleworth)
Below: Laying the final piece of turf at Hilton Park (Bob Shuttleworth)

Below: Being introduced to Mayor Alderman Battersby by chairman James Hilton ahead of the first game at Hilton Park in August 1947 (Bob Shuttleworth)

Above: Widnes players and officials ahead of the 1950 Challenge Cup final. I've got the ball!

Right: On the ball again before the 1950 final.

Left: Celebrating Widnes' rich Challenge Cup history with club greats, including Joe Egan (left) and Vince Karalius (second left).

Above: With my great staff at St Peter's.

Right: Meeting Jimmy Saville with the Leigh schoolboys team at Wembley (Bob Shuttleworth).

Below: At Wembley on a Leigh supporters' club trip.

Above: A great honour and a lovely surprise: the naming of the Tommy Sale Stand at Hilton Park.

Left: My good friend Colin Hutton presents me with a memento after being inducted onto the Rugby Football League's Roll of Honour.

Above: With my family after being presented with an award for voluntary achievement by Wigan Metropolitan Borough Council. Left-right: Fiona, Evelyne, Ronnie, me, Fiona's husband Terry, mayor Bernard Holt and his daughter & consort Susan Evans, Jean.

Above: With Billy Boston and Mayor Joan Hurst after being awarded the Freedom of the Borough of Wigan, a magnificent honour of which I am very proud.

Left: Leading the Leigh team out ahead of the Northern Ford Premiership Grand Final in 2000. Coach Paul Terzis is behind me.

Below: My 90th birthday party. I'm very lucky to have such a wonderful family.

Above: The naming of Sale Way - an honour for time immemorial.

Left: Timekeeping has been a great way to stay involved with the club and game I love.

*

Chapter Sixteen

To experience what I did in my first season at Widnes, considering where I had been at the start of the 1949-50 campaign, was almost beyond my comprehension. It really was the most amazing Indian summer. I had been on the scrapheap at Leigh, written off completely and all but forced into premature retirement. The lifeline Widnes threw me came as a surprise but I grabbed it with both hands and the autumn of my career was a memorable one indeed.

I played all 25 games before the end of the season after my arrival, a run that culminated with the Challenge Cup final, and scored 12 tries along the way. It was a wonderful sequence that I did not want to end but, of course, all good things must eventually.

I missed playing when I finally came to retire, but I knew when my time was up. The signs were there throughout my second season at Widnes as I was consigned mostly to the A team and suffered the first serious injury of my career. I played on until the end of the 1950-51 campaign but then decided to hang up my boots. I was almost 33 and not the player I had been. My fitness was still good but my pace had started to go. The game is only worth playing if you are enjoying it and as opponents started to catch me from behind with greater regularity, my enthusiasm was knocked. I'd always had a bit of speed and it was a sad day when I realised it was no longer there. I was starting to struggle and was not enjoying playing as much as I used to.

It was a shame because I actually went into the season with great confidence. Like the rest of the team, I was keen to maintain the momentum from the previous May's Wembley visit. I couldn't wait to get going and really enjoyed a pre-season friendly win over my old Leigh colleagues in which I scored a try, went close to grabbing another and then beat three or four men to set up Percy Davies. Unfortunately that was as good as it got as we made a terrible start to the season proper, losing six of our first seven games. The only game we won was a Lancashire Cup tie against Salford and I missed that. I was back in the side for the second leg but we couldn't hang on to our lead and went out on aggregate.

My last try for Widnes came in a slender 5-3 defeat at Hull in September 1950. I managed to show enough pace to touch down in the corner after a fine move instigated by Davies and Charlie Reynolds but it was not enough. Hull's try in that game was controversial, coming in the 45th minute of the first half, but any injustice we felt over referee Charlie Appleton's timekeeping was offset by the fact we squandered several good chances to win.

After that I was left out of the first team for a couple of months and it came as a surprise to some when I was eventually recalled for a trip to Oldham in the November. The *Widnes Weekly News* thought I had already bid a "graceful adieu" to the senior game when I was named in the side, even though I had not given up and produced some good tryscoring performances in the A team. Unfortunately the same paper was not particularly impressed with what it saw of me on my return. "It is not heartless to say Sale's days are numbered," read its report of the game, which we lost 3-0 after a first-minute try.

Nevertheless, I kept my place for the next game against Wigan and actually opened the scoring by kicking a penalty. That hadn't been in the script, given my past indifference towards goalkicking, but it at least gave me another two points to my Widnes tally – my last, as it turned out. I could have had another couple but, more like my old kicking self, I missed with another attempt. We lost that game, as we did our next at Belle Vue Rangers and sadly that proved the end for me in the Widnes first team. I still made the squad list a few times but never got into the final 13 again.

Colin Hutton, who was one of my closest friends at Widnes, also began to lose his place around the same time and before the end of the season had moved to Hull. That was a move that rejuvenated him and I was very pleased for him when he went on to play in a Championship play-off final. When I think of all my best memories of Widnes, Colin is always in them. We not only played well together but enjoyed each other's company off the field. He was a great lad and I was surprised when he left but he was a good signing for Hull and later served the game well as a coach and administrator, primarily at Hull KR, where he is now president.

I'll never know if I might have got more chances in that last season had I not dislocated my elbow in an A team game at Workington in January 1951. It put me out for a couple of months, the only prolonged injury-enforced absence I ever suffered, and when I returned there was little of the season remaining. It was a very painful injury too, and led to a lot of embarrassment at the Cumberland hospital I was taken to for treatment. I was looked after by a nice-looking female doctor and I remember thinking how lovely she was as I lay back and they put me under anaesthetic. After they put my elbow right and I came round, I became aware that the club director who had accompanied me was laughing hysterically. As I slowly came to my senses I asked him what he was laughing at. He said I'd been saying some funny things while I'd been dazed. I thought I must have been swearing but he told me it was nothing like that. Apparently I'd been saying, repeatedly, how beautiful the doctor was! I turned red when I saw her again.

As frustrating as that injury was at the time, I was actually very fortunate that, apart from the odd bump or bruise, I got through the rest of my career relatively unscathed. I looked after myself physically throughout my career and cringed when I saw how lazy or careless some other players were. I can think of a few that were so reckless in how they treated themselves that they were lucky to play the game. They probably wouldn't survive if they were playing nowadays. Rugby league, particularly in Super League, is very robust, the players are bigger and the collisions more punishing. The game is certainly a lot harder and, to be honest, I'm not sure if I would have much enjoyed playing nowadays either.

One thing is for sure, fit as I was, my training regime would not have been sufficient for rugby league in 2010. When I look at modern players the first thing I notice is how big their arms and thighs are. These men, backs as well as forwards, are huge. In my day nearly all the backs were skinny like me. We never did any weights and I concentrated on sprint training for my fitness. My reasoning was that I felt you needed pace as a back to give you an edge. These days players focus more on building muscles and strength conditioning. There are obviously still some natural speedsters out there but generally I don't think the game is as fast now. Players aren't as quick as they were because they are carrying more weight. The trade-off is that they are far tougher.

When I watch some matches now, I do wonder how I ever played the game. It is so different and I don't think I could have lasted. But that is not to say players of my era weren't every bit as committed. I seldom went out onto the field holding back and most others were the same. When you are in the thick of it you tend to forget your lumps and bumps and battle on. Generally if you go in 100% you tend to come out okay. It is when you start holding back or hesitating that you run a greater risk of getting injured.

The only time I can ever recall being slightly hesitant was in my first game back after dislocating my elbow. I'd been sidelined for several weeks and our physio, Frank Tobin, had been very strict with me. I'd wanted to play again much sooner but he'd ruled me out. Only when he felt I was ready could I play and when that time came he took me into his room, pulled my arm out and bent it this way and that. He then gave me the all-clear but I knew if I hurt it again he'd insist I was out of the firing line for longer. He was right of course and he was a very good physio. He had to do what was right for the team.

By this time the season was coming to an end and, having already realised my performances were on the wane, I began to contemplate a non-playing future. In preparation for the end of my career I'd already qualified as a coach and when an offer came from Wigan to take charge of their A team the following season, it seemed too good an opportunity to turn down. I apologised to Widnes, because I still felt I owed them a lot, but it seemed the best move for everyone concerned. I left with a heavy heart but I feel I at least left a pretty good parting gift in my younger brother John. During my final year I'd persuaded the club to give John a trial and his career was just getting started as mine ended. He went on to play 161 games and kick 213 goals over seven seasons with the Chemics.

John and I actually played together in the A team in what was to be my final game in a Widnes shirt in April 1951. We beat Wigan A 27-9 and both played really well, I scoring a try and John kicking two goals. It was a good way to finish and I announced my retirement to the lads in the bath afterwards. A few of them tried to talk me out of it but my mind was made up and I wrote to the club to inform them of my intentions soon after. It brought to an end a wonderful chapter in my life. I played 34 times and scored 13 tries for the Widnes first team. Unfortunately none of the nine games I played in 1950-51 were in a winning side, and the season as a whole proved one of struggle for the club, but I look back on my years at Naughton Park with nothing but immense satisfaction. I left feeling fulfilled and with a career I could really look back on with pride.

But as much as I loved my stint at Widnes, I must admit it was still strange to have to play against Leigh from time to time. The first occasion was the most surreal. I'd been at Widnes less than two months and it just didn't feel right to be using the visiting dressing room at Kirkhall Lane. I was also given a great reception by the home supporters even though I was determined to show them what they were missing. I enjoyed the game and think I gave a good account of myself although, after having four tries disallowed as a team, we needed a late Percy Davies drop goal to salvage a 2-2 draw. Games against Leigh were always something I relished as I felt I had a point to prove, even in friendlies. I was especially pleased with the try I scored against them in the warm-up game prior to the 1950-51 season.

The other notable thing about that drawn game at Leigh was the toughness of the conditions. It was really icy and the pitch had been covered with straw beforehand to help it beat the frost. That was not atypical. It also got awfully muddy at certain times of year and one aspect of today's game I know I would have liked is the summer season. I enjoyed playing in all weathers and these days I do miss the traditional winter fixtures, but I would still have loved to have played on hard pitches in the sun. They would really have suited my game. I played in baking hot conditions in the Persian Gulf during the War and enjoyed it considerably. It would have been fantastic to have played during the summer in England too.

I always tried to keep my discipline on the field and I treated referees with the utmost respect. I found it just doesn't pay to swear at or curse them. Referees are human and can make mistakes like anyone else and you have to remember that. Losing your temper with them merely antagonises them and it is usually your team that suffers. I remember one, whose name escapes me now, who was notorious for his discipline and could send you off just for looking at him. You had to treat officials like him courteously. Throughout my career I would always approach referees in a nice manner and address them as "sir". I think such an attitude serves people well in the game and I can think of some modern players that need to learn that.

Paul Rowley has been a great servant to Leigh and I hold him in very high regard, but when he was a player discipline was an area where he did occasionally let himself down. I remember one game when he called a ref a really nasty name within five minutes and was sent off straightaway. It was stupid. When a referee makes a decision, no matter what you do or say he is not going to change his mind, so there is no point giving penalties away by arguing. It frustrates me when I see the current Leigh side doing that. I have yet to see a referee go back on his decision. It doesn't happen.

I can remember one occasion when my attitude towards referees did our team a favour. We were playing Barrow and attacking on their 25-yard line when I broke through from a good pass. I thought I was certain to score and sidestepped my way towards the posts but Charlie Appleton had different ideas and blew up for a forward pass. It was never forward in a million years and I couldn't believe it but I kept my cool, even though we had quite clearly been robbed. I knew Charlie's mind was made up and he would not change it no matter what I said, so I voiced my displeasure in as polite a manner as possible. "Excuse me sir? Forward pass?" I asked calmly. He replied firmly and without a moment's hesitation. "Yes," he said, and ordered us to scrum down.

Yet Charlie, who was a small chap from Warrington, was actually one of the better referees of his day despite this and the aforementioned Hull timekeeping episode. He usually read the game well and deep down he knew he had got it wrong. He admitted as much after the game. He came up to me in the bar and quietly said he realised he'd blown the whistle too quickly. He said he thought I was right after all. I appreciated that and thanked him, although I did add the decision had still probably cost us the game.

I thought that was the end of the matter until Charlie refereed us again in a game against Rochdale a few weeks later. This time I benefited after I was thrown a pass on the Rochdale 25-yard line and dropped it. I was about to curse my luck but the ball took a lucky bounce and jumped back into my arms. Even though I was expecting a whistle at any moment, I instinctively played on and ran in to score.

Amazingly, that whistle never came and the try was given. I couldn't believe I'd got away with such a blatant knock-on but as I walked back past Charlie he let on that he'd seen exactly what had happened. "That's us quits now," he muttered out of the corner of his mouth.

Something else I picked up at Widnes was a new nickname. Whilst my Leigh team-mates knew me as 'The Diver', at Widnes the name 'Gluke' caught on. It was short for glucose and came about because I used to spend time before every match mixing and then knocking back my own energy drinks. I devised these concoctions myself, working on the theory that glucose is absorbed into the bloodstream much quicker than ordinary sugar and can therefore deliver a sharp energy boost just before a game. I drank them without fail and did my best to persuade the others to do so too, but it never really caught on, although a few tried it. Sometimes I added the odd drop of sherry to try to tempt them but they still thought it took too long to mix to bother with. I did not let that deter me though. I used to swear by my glucose drinks and I never put any alcohol in mine, despite what the lads thought! I always had a bottle in my pocket and would drink it 30 minutes or so before a game.

The dressing room banter is just one of the things I miss from my playing days. I loved every minute of my career and I wish I could get out there and do it all over again. Saturdays were our matchdays back then and they really couldn't come quickly enough. As soon as one ended I started looking forward to the next. I just wanted to get the week done as quickly as possible.

Even after retiring I was unable to resist offers to turn out in various one-off friendlies. I remember scoring a hat-trick of tries in one charity game when I was 49 and I was still at it at 72. That was for a Leigh team in a game of half-rugby union, half-rugby league against a side from Tyldesley. I heard plenty of comments like, "Get off Saley, you'll be dropping dead," but I battled on until I had to be carried off. I loved playing that much. No matter how much I continued to love rugby league after I retired, nothing ever replaced that thrill of running with ball in hand.

*

Chapter Seventeen

Rugby league and its players have benefited enormously from the advent of full-time professionalism but I wouldn't have wanted it in my era. I always wanted a good job from which I could secure a living for the rest of my life. It must be great to be a full-time professional but playing careers are only short. You have to have something else lined up for when you retire and I was always conscious of that. I entered the world of work two days after I left school at 14, taking that awful job at the mill, and never left it. I never claimed the dole in my life and even now I still keep myself busy helping out at the rugby club.

I had a steady job throughout my time as a rugby player and regarded my wages from the game as a very handy bonus. There were no contracts in those days and all players received the same money. At both Leigh and Widnes the rate was £8 for a win and about £3 for a loss. I think the richer clubs such as Leeds paid their players about £15 a win but what we got was fairly standard. When pay time came all the wage packets were thrown onto the training benches and you just had to go and collect one.

In my early days at Leigh I was once done out of my money. We had been beaten at Mather Lane and were due to be paid £3.3s. Harry Prescott, the secretary, used to come round and hand out the money from his back pocket but as the youngest in the team I was always left until last. When he finally reached me he claimed to have run out of money and asked if I would instead accept 30 shillings' worth of club draw tickets (about £1.50 in modern money). Being rather naive I agreed but of course there was not a single winner among them. I was left with absolutely nothing. I was disappointed but didn't get any sympathy from the mate I went out with that night. He just told me, quite bluntly, that after such a performance I'd got exactly what I deserved!

When I first joined Leigh the thought of trying to negotiate a signing-on fee never occurred to me. In those days I was excited to be joining the club and just wanted to play. By the time I moved to Widnes I was considerably more worldly-wise and managed to secure a £100 lump sum. I put that to good use by buying my first car, a Ford Popular. It was something I realised I needed soon after starting training with the Chemics. To get there I had to catch a bus to Warrington and then another to Widnes and we trained twice a week. It was arduous. That car made a big difference and it served me well for many years. It was a great runner and we got many family holidays out of it.

That might have been the first car I owned but driving was not a new experience. I'd actually passed my test shortly before being called up for national service, in June 1939. I told the examiner that day that I needed to pass because I was about to join up with the Army and, rather sportingly, he let me through despite clipping a kerb.

Chapter Seventeen

And if driving tests were easier then, drink driving laws were non-existent. I remember driving home after one particularly heavy night in Preston and how I made it I'll never know. I'd gone up there with a friend called Bert Partington, who came from Leigh but I only met him during the War. Like most towns, Leigh gave a lot of men to the War but, serving first in Scotland and later joining a regiment from Kent, I encountered few of my hometown contemporaries during my years of service. Bert was an exception. I met him in Palestine and we got on very well. He was commissioned soon after me and linked up with a different battery of the same regiment. I didn't actually see him again after that until the end of the War but I got to hear that he had been blinded by a flashlight. When I got home I made an effort to meet up with him. We became firm friends and regularly went out for drinks. The trip to Preston came after we arranged to meet up with another of our comrades from overseas. We had a right good bash-up and it really was a miracle I got home after that. I shudder at the thought of that now.

I had many a good night out in Leigh as a rugby player but some unhappy ones as well. That was the price of being a familiar face in the town. If you had a good game the people were great but if you'd had a bad one, your life was hell. You couldn't enjoy yourself. I got sick of that and so did my wife. The worst time, not surprisingly, was after I disgraced myself by dropping that ball against Halifax. What I was doing going out that night I don't know. I should have just gone straight home.

Things changed, however, after I went to Widnes. The Leigh folk were no longer bothered how I'd played then and I could go out and have a pint no problem. I enjoyed the craic. I used to go out regularly but never on Fridays before a game. Saturdays and Sundays were my days and I'd happily go down to the George & Dragon for a drink or two. I always kept things in moderation, though. Being a fitness fanatic I was never a heavy drinker and smoked only the odd cigar.

I considered running a pub myself for a while. It was one of the options I explored after the War as I looked around for something that paid better than my old job in the parks department. It was a path that had been well trodden by Leigh rugby players in the past because of the involvement of George Shaw's brewery in the club. The brewery had always been great supporters of Leigh and when they owned the old Mather Lane ground, which they sold during the War, a lot of players got pubs in return for playing in the team.

George Shaw's were very prominent in the town. I reckon you could have walked the mile or so from Butt's Bridge to the Turnpike in the town centre and passed about 10 of their pubs on the way. They were very distinctive with their doors and window frames all painted blue. The club secretary, Harry Prescott, had one and so did a handful of players. I put in for one too but was overlooked.

As it turned out, that was for the best. Had I gone down that route I might never have stumbled into what proved my dream profession; teaching. I loved teaching. I got involved quite by chance but once I started I didn't want to stop. Most days I couldn't get to school quickly enough and I carried on long after retirement age. I taught for 33 years, 13 as headmaster, and relished every minute of it. I spent my entire career at St Peter's in Leigh and I am very proud of everything I achieved there. Given the start I had in life and the dead-end nature of my first job, I really am very lucky how things turned out in the end.

*

Chapter Eighteen

The building of Hilton Park was not only one of my greatest accomplishments but also an incredible turning point in my life. It was whilst working on the ground that I got into a chance conversation with one of the other volunteers and my entire outlook changed.

I'd never considered teaching until this man got talking to me. He was a strong supporter of the club and the boss of the job centre on Railway Road. He asked about what I normally did for a living and I told him I was usually based at the park at Pennington Hall. It was a nice job but the money wasn't good enough. It had been quite a comedown after being a lieutenant in the Army and I kept having to work overtime to make up a decent wage. I told him I'd had enough and was actively looking for something else. I was also undertaking correspondence courses in maths and English to broaden my options.

It was then he suggested giving teaching a go. He told me there was a huge shortage of teachers following the War and that a new emergency scheme had been set up to recruit more. Rather than it taking the usual three years, people could now qualify after just one 12-month course. I was immediately interested and thought I should apply. Initially I thought I could teach PE.

I went to see this man in his office the next day. He even filled out the application form for me. We sent it off and soon after I was asked to go to Warrington for an interview and to sit an exam. I passed and was offered a place at college in Bamber Bridge, near Preston. The course began a few months later. By this time I had moved on to another job with the corporation, developing the Marsh Playing Fields. This was another satisfying project. Following the success of Hilton Park, I was asked to supervise the transformation of a large patch of rough ground, donated to the town by the Marsh family, into a lasting resource for the community. It went very well and was nearing completion when I left to begin the course.

I was well supported by my wife and my mother as I embarked on my new career, although my father was rubbish as usual. The course went very well. The college had been an American camp during the War and had a big dining room with huts all the way around. It was well suited to the purpose and I learned a lot. I specialised in PE but I realised primary education was where I wanted to focus and so I prepared to teach all subjects. After finishing I found a job close to home, at St Peter's Church of England Junior School, almost straightaway.

When I began I could never have envisaged that I'd stay at one school for so long but I really never had cause to leave. The Plank Lane area of Leigh might be a bit rough around the edges and there were some tough kids but it was a wonderful school with a great staff. I really enjoyed my time there.

Chapter Eighteen

I commenced duties on March 7, 1949 and I remember it vividly. The headmaster introduced me to the whole school in front of an assembly on my first morning. He knew a lot of the children might recognise me as Tommy Sale the rugby player and he wanted to make sure the ground rules were laid down from day one.

"You may know this gentleman," he said firmly. "A lot of you lads will know who he is. He is Tommy Sale. But don't let me hear any of you call him Tommy Sale. It is Mr Sale from now on!"

Yet the kids actually liked the fact I was a rugby player. This became clear when, just over a year later, they gave me a wonderful and heart-warming reception when I returned to work two days after playing the game of my life to take Widnes to Wembley. When I arrived at school on the Monday morning I found them all lined up inside the gates waiting for me. They cheered like mad as I walked through. That was a great feeling and the kids then got to enjoy some of the build-up to the final as the local press came round to take pictures of me in the classroom. Unfortunately Warrington ensured there was to be no follow-up and the reception I received after the final was totally different.

Prior to that the children had been great with me in my first year in the job. My start coincided with my lowest ebb in rugby, when I was out of the picture at Leigh, and it gave me a new focus. I really settled in well at St Peter's. I knew even then that I had a lot for which to thank the man from the job centre. Our conversation at Hilton Park had changed my life.

There was also a great community spirit around the school and church and one other story connecting St Peter's with that 1950 semi-final readily springs to mind. It involved the dramatics society and a production on the evening of the match that I couldn't get out of, despite the game's importance. They were a good group and regularly put on performances at Wigan Road Methodist Church, a venue they used because St Peter's didn't have its own hall with a stage. I was a keen member but amateur dramatics was not what I wanted to be doing in the hours after the biggest game of my life. I had initially been excited when the vicar told me we were entering a competition at Briarcroft Hall but was immediately deflated when given the date. I said I didn't think I'd be able to make it. I said I was due to play for Widnes in a big semi-final that afternoon and if we won there was no telling what state I would be in by the evening. I added I was also likely to be pretty disinterested if we lost. Yet all that fell on deaf ears. I was simply told I'd be alright on the night and not to worry! Stage fright was actually the least of my worries.

So, with apparently no choice in the matter, I agreed to take part in the show, but told the vicar that on his head be it if I was not on top form. Of course we then went and won the game and, after scoring twice and being carried off the field, it was the farthest thing from my mind as I set off on a celebratory circuit of the pubs of Wigan with the lads. Not surprisingly, the ale was really flowing. Every pub we went into was full of Widnes fans and it seemed they all wanted to buy me a drink. I then stopped off for one in Leigh on my way to St Peter's and again found people steadfastly against the idea of me buying my own drinks. Not surprisingly, by 9 o'clock I was well away.

Everyone could tell I was half-cut by the time I arrived at the hall. "Good God, look at the state of him," I heard people say. Yet I could hardly have cared less. "Don't worry, I'm alright," I said and confidently took to the stage. It did not go well. Everyone was so upset about me that they seemed to keep forgetting their lines. I jumped in and said them for them, but then often found I couldn't remember my own. I found the whole thing very funny, even though no-one else was amused.

Afterwards the vicar apologised to the adjudicator, an Austrian lady called Gertrude Liebrich, for my performance. "You must excuse Mr Sale," he said. "He played in a semi-final this afternoon and in a few weeks time he will be playing at Wembley."

"Oh," she replied. "Is he so good a tennis player?"

*

Chapter Nineteen

In the 20 years of teaching I enjoyed before becoming headmaster the thing that stands out in my mind as my proudest achievement is the work I did with slow-learning children. This was something I was pushed into by the head at the time, and something I was not initially pleased about. In those days teaching so-called 'backward' pupils – a term completely unacceptable in today's society – was a job generally handed to the worst teachers and, in the opinion of our head, that was most definitely me. I was determined to prove him wrong and wanted to give it a good go.

I was given a class of 14 slow-learners and I put my heart and soul in the challenge. Yet it was far tougher than I could have imagined and after a few months of getting nowhere I came to the conclusion I was not qualified enough for the job. The convention of handing this task to teachers considered the weakest was all wrong. It required more skills than anything else and I was inadequately prepared. It had been far easier teaching brighter children, who can pick things up and, to some degree, teach themselves. I went to tell the head this but I did not want to give up. I did some research and found a course at Edge Hill college from which I thought I could benefit enormously. I suggested I should be spared to attend what was a 12-month course.

The head did not agree and was reluctant to let me leave but I managed to persuade him. I argued he could easily find a supply to cover while I was away. It proved every bit as worthwhile as I had hoped for. I learnt more in those 12 months than I could have done in 12 years of normal teaching. Where it really proved informative was in allowing students to visit specialist schools to observe all the different methods used in teaching children with learning difficulties. We went to all manner of schools, each of which dealt with a different disability, and I made copious notes. I had a file several inches thick full of papers and photographs. The main thing I learned was the importance of diagnostics; in other words the understanding of why children were how they were and then working out how to get the best out of them.

When I went back to St Peter's I was far better equipped. I knew how to deal with the children, how to communicate better and how to calm them down in moments of anxiety. My methods worked extremely well and as a result I earned a reputation. After a short while a teaching college in Culcheth started sending their students to observe my classes and I was asked to go there and give lectures. Undertaking that course at Edge Hill was undoubtedly the best thing I ever did in teaching. Not only was it very rewarding but I have no doubt the work I did following it was instrumental in my eventual securing of the headship.

Implementing new ideas, such as those I picked up on that course, was something that came naturally. I always tried to be as innovative as possible in my teaching. One of my hobbies at the time was keeping butterflies and I found that lent itself well to education. I used to buy eggs from a place in Yorkshire and put them in big fish tanks with twigs and leaves. I would take them to school so the children could watch the caterpillars hatching, growing and eventually metamorphosising into butterflies, some of which were huge. The other teachers hadn't seen anyone teach like that before but I thought it was a good way to show children what happened in nature.

I also kept bees for a while. That was something I was introduced to by my tutor at Bamber Bridge, who did it professionally. He said he could get a hive for any students that might be interested and, knowing that it would look good to have outside interests, I decided to give it a go. I found it very interesting and used to love the honey. It produced about a gallon of it in the summer months. It was a painful experience at first however, as whenever I went into the hive I got stung on my forehead. I couldn't understand why and after a while I asked the expert. He said the Brylcreem in my hair was attracting them to my head! After that I started wearing a cap.

I was appointed headmaster at St Peter's in February 1969 and took up the position two months later. It was the culmination of many years of hard work but the busiest were yet to come. Being head was stressful at times but I wouldn't have had it any other way. Running a school in such an area was quite a challenge and there were many difficult children to deal with, but I relished it.

Throughout my tenure I insisted on strict discipline. If I had nothing else, I certainly had order. I used the cane from the day I started to the day I left and I had no qualms about it. I always said manners maketh man and I made sure the children were always well behaved. Any that stepped out of line were dealt with. It made for a good teaching environment and the results were positive.

Chapter Nineteen

Corporal punishment is, of course, considered cruel nowadays and I feel standards of behaviour amongst the young have dropped. I couldn't have taught without discipline and I wonder how today's teachers cope. I visited a school recently and was shocked when a child jumped up and answered back to his teacher. "I'm not doing it," he snapped. I'd have liked to have seen him try that in my day. I'd have flattened him! I told the teacher that but she said there was nothing she could do. Sometimes even if teachers speak to children in a certain way now they can get into trouble.

My methods may have been out of line with modern thinking but I know I made my mark. I was with the chief education officer of Wigan Metropolitan Borough at a function at Leigh town hall not too long ago and whenever he introduced me to someone else he would add, "This gentleman ran one of the best primary schools in the whole Wigan borough." When they asked why he'd say it was because I had discipline. I wouldn't let children walk past me in the corridor without saying "excuse me". If they did walk straight past I'd let them go for about 30 yards and then call them back to ask what they'd forgotten. If there was a piece of paper on the floor I'd tell them to pick it up. Basically, if I said jump, they asked how high.

I know if I was working today and carried on as I did then I'd probably end up in jail. Times have moved on but I do worry where children are learning their manners from if it is not at school, because so many homes are dysfunctional. It upsets me how cheeky some children are; no 'pleases', no 'thank yous'. Manners should start from home but if parents are not doing their jobs, the role of the school is vital. I do believe this lack of discipline is the root of a lot of problems in society. After Hilton Park closed down in 2008 the Leigh rugby club had some trouble with vandals. When the perpetrators were eventually caught, at 2am one morning, it turned out the youngest of them was about 12 and the eldest 16. What on earth are kids that age doing out at such a time, behaving so badly? Parents need to be made to take responsibility. I had a father who never had the slightest hesitation in disciplining me when I erred, particularly when he'd had a drink, but admittedly he's an extreme example.

The school had a good reputation but I did have a number of run-ins with parents over the use of corporal punishment. They couldn't claim they weren't warned, however, because I wrote to every parent when their child joined us from the infant school making clear what our policies were. I made it compulsory that they signed a declaration stating they understood this before their child was accepted. If there were any subsequent complaints I'd remind them of what they had signed and dig it out of the filing cabinet if necessary. I'd say they were always free to take their children elsewhere but, knowing how good the school was, more often than not they'd back down.

Unfortunately there were occasions when things did get out of hand. I had more than one fight with a dad. One time I was rugby-tackled from behind by an irate father and bashed my head, so I kept my wits about me after that. When another father took a swing at me in my office I made sure he only did so once because I grabbed him and put him through the door. Mothers were more problematic, however. When a man takes a pop at you, you can react and do something about it but what do you do when a woman does? It was very difficult.

When it came to the cane, though, I always felt I was fair. I often see my old pupils out and about in Leigh and sometimes they'll come and remind me about the time I gave them the stick. I reply simply by telling them that if I did do that to them then they must have deserved it. Usually they'll agree. By and large the children knew where they stood. If they behaved, everything was fine.

Sadly some kids are going to misbehave whatever discipline you try to impose. The worst one I encountered in my time burnt the school down. That was a horrific experience. I couldn't believe it when I was called and told the school was ablaze. One of the boys had somehow got hold of some paint from a cupboard and lit it, with devastating consequences. Large parts of the place were gutted and I had the tough task of keeping everybody together. For two-and-a-half years our classes were scattered across three different locations, with two in the hall at Sacred Heart and two at Scott Street youth club, while the school was rebuilt. I had to keep flitting from one place to another. It was terrible. It was quite early into my headship too, so a huge test. I was reassured by the governors, who constantly gave me their backing. They said they were glad to have me in charge and that gave me the encouragement I needed to get through.

The lad that did it had been a real nuisance for a long time. He was about 10 or 11 and had been in trouble regularly throughout his time at the school. He was a real naughty devil and I'd caned him many times. After the fire I told his mother that it was not right for him to remain at the school. Putting it mildly, I said that next time I saw him I was likely to take advantage. Thankfully she agreed and took him elsewhere. I was glad to see the back of him. On the positive side, at least we got a nice new building out of it.

Another serious incident in my time involved a teenage girl coming into school to attack a teacher with a knife. We only narrowly averted a major tragedy. The girl was about 16 and had been taking a shortcut through the playground. When one of the teachers told her this was unacceptable, she responded with a barrage of obscenities. She was asked to moderate her language in front of the children but the situation became quite heated, another nearby teacher got involved and I was called for. I wanted to call the police but first had to get her away from the children and asked her to come inside. I sat her in my office while I made the call but she panicked and as soon as I placed the receiver down she made a run for the door. I jumped up and blocked her off but she started swearing and hitting me. I restrained her and forced her back into the chair and then told her she would not be leaving until the police arrived. Until that moment, because of her appearance, I'd actually assumed she was a boy. It was only as I'd got close up that I began to think otherwise. I asked for confirmation but she swore back once again and told me, rather crudely, there was only one way I'd be able to find out her sex. Charming! As I've mentioned, it was a rough area.

The day ended with a trip to court and the girl was given a suspended £50 fine. We thought that would be the end of the matter but about a week later I was taking morning assembly when the secretary came and tapped me on the shoulder. She told me the same girl had come into school to ask if she could speak in private to the teacher she initially argued with. They had gone into my office. I was alarmed and ran down the corridor. I burst into the office and was confronted with the sight of the girl brandishing a dagger, preparing to lunge at the teacher's stomach. I raced in and grabbed the outstretched arm of my colleague and pulled her out of harm's way. The girl thrust the knife forward in my direction but I sidestepped her advance, grabbed her wrist and twisted her arm up behind her back. I then forced her into the foyer, where there was more room, and wrestled the knife from her grasp, telling her I'd break her arm if she didn't let go. I meant that too. Once I'd got it I threw it as far as possible down the corridor. At this point I noticed out of the corner of my eye that the children were about to be led out of the hall after assembly. No-one else had any idea of what was going on so I yelled for them to be kept back in. The secretary called for the police but the girl continued to struggle so I had to pin her down on the deck for 15 minutes until they arrived.

The sad thing was that after all that the girl still got away with it. I was disgusted with that. It could have been a serious crime. If I hadn't gone into the room, the teacher would have been stabbed and we could have had a murder on our hands. I got there just in time.

Yet for every bad kid there were plenty of good ones. One I remember very well was Clive Powell, who later became known as the pop singer Georgie Fame and had number one hits in the mid-1960s with *Yeh Yeh, Get Away* and *The Ballad of Bonnie & Clyde*. He was probably my most famous old boy. He was very theatrical and musical at school, a natural performer. Every year the cable works used to ask me to arrange a children's party concert and Georgie, who loved singing and could also play the piano or organ, relished it. He'd never hesitate to get up whenever I said it was his turn to play. His father worked at the cable works and he loved to show off in front of him. He was a lovely lad but also a real character. One time he tried to get out of an exam by coming into school in the morning with his arm in a sling. He fooled his teacher but he didn't fool me. I could see there was no plaster on it so asked him to come to me. When he did I grabbed his arm and pulled it out of the sling. He did not even wince and so I told him he had to sit the exam like everyone else.

I always liked him and was really pleased that he did so well for himself in life. He made good money from his music. I remember him dropping in unannounced at the team hotel when Leigh got to Wembley in 1971. He'd just done a gig nearby and so popped in to see me and the players. He found out which room I was in and I was pleasantly surprised when I answered the door to him. He still has high regard for Leigh and speaks of me a lot, which is nice. He sent me a nice letter on my 90th birthday and it was read out as a surprise at my party. We also met recently at the Leigh Miners Welfare Club when he did a concert for the rugby league's Benevolent Fund.

Another brilliant musician I taught was Andy Prior, of 'Big Band' fame. Andy, who played the trombone at school and was a big fan of Frank Sinatra, initially went into music with his dad. He then carved out quite a reputation in the jazz and swing music worlds after setting up his own band in the 1980s. He has toured this country and America and, in recent years, fronted his own television show.

He was another who enjoyed the concerts we put on at St Peter's, many of which often involved me playing the organ. I used to love music and sometimes we'd put on shows with as many as five of us all playing together. They were great times and among the many memories I cherish from my time at the school. In all, I had a wonderful time there. The knife incident occurred just months before I retired in August 1982 but not even that could take the gloss off it.

I was very sad when the time came for me to leave and I missed it terribly afterwards. The only days I found boring in all my time there were the holidays. I was extremely happy at St Peter's and everyone was very good to me. It was not only the school I loved but the church too. I attended it every Sunday, served on its council for 32 years and had many good friends there.

I continue to reap the rewards from my career as it earned me a good pension. I really do feel very lucky to have got to where I am from where I began. Given the start I had in life, my path from the mill to the headship is something of which I am very proud. Teaching was the perfect job for me and becoming head topped it off. I still visit St Peter's from time to time, for things such as garden parties or Christmas fayres, and that is always enjoyable. How times have changed though. I've mentioned how the kids are far cheekier now but that would not be my only problem. Computers were only just coming into schools when I left, now they're everywhere. I wouldn't know where to start!

*

Chapter Twenty

I was fully committed to St Peter's and devoted huge swathes of my spare time to rugby league, but that did not stop me dipping my toes into the world of business as well. In fact, to a lot of people in Leigh I was probably better known as a former rugby player-turned-sweet shop owner than I was as a teacher.

Again, it was something that came about by chance. I was very happy as a teacher and was not particularly looking for any extra income when the opportunity came along. In fact, if I didn't like chocolate so much it probably wouldn't have happened at all.

The shop I took over was a very popular one in the town centre, close to where the Spinning Jenny pub now stands. It was always busy, particularly at lunch and tea times. It benefitted from being so close to the old cinema and it also used to get a lot of business from commuters, especially those from the cable works. I was a regular customer myself and often nipped in for a bar of chocolate as I went through town. The shopkeeper was a very friendly chap and we'd always have a little chat whenever I went in. Usually this was about something inconsequential, so I couldn't believe my ears when he asked me one day if I wanted to buy the business. I thought I must have misheard, but he was serious. He told me that he was retiring and looking to sell up. He wanted £800 for the shop.

With a steady job already and a happy family life to boot, I had no reason to take it on. But my curiosity was aroused and I knew it was potentially a good earner. The shop was one of the best of its kind in Leigh and it was in a good location. I knew it would mean long hours, as it did good business from 6am to 10pm, but I was still young and fit and that was not such an obstacle. To run it around my existing work I'd obviously have to rely on staff to keep it ticking over but I thought it was manageable. My wife was not interested in getting involved but she had no objection and so, after some thought, I decided to give it a go and went to the bank for a loan.

It was everything I hoped for at first. It started earning immediately and I soon had to take on more staff. At the busy times I had to have two or even three assistants in and I had eight on the rota in total. We were known for selling sweets but cigarettes and tobacco actually made the most money. It was a lucrative business and had I stuck at it and concentrated on it fully I would probably have been able to retire a lot earlier than I did.

Unfortunately I was unable to give it the attention it required and my staff took advantage. I was at school during the day and then spent a lot of the rest of my time at Leigh rugby league club, where by this time I was on the board. I was just away too much and consequently I was being robbed left, right and centre. Some of the women that worked for me were taking 10 shillings out of every sale.

Someone would come to buy something for 12 and six, for example, and only two and six would get punched into the till. The other 10 bob would end up in the assistant's pocket. When I suspected something fishy was going on I got the police onto it and twice they caught people, quite literally, with their fingers in the till.

I found this hugely disheartening and in the end, after about six years, I decided to pack it in. In fact, I was so upset that I gave the shop away. Financially, that was foolish but I just lost the will. I could have tightened up procedures and carried on, and the result would probably have been a very tidy living. Yet as long as I continued to enjoy my rugby and my teaching, and I had no intention of giving either of them up, it was unlikely I'd ever be able to devote enough time to it.

Looking at the sales figures I was foolish to let it go but it turned out for the best. Had I continued with the shop I don't think I'd have been made a headmaster and consequently I wouldn't be living on such a good pension now. I also wouldn't have had the same job satisfaction. I think I did the right thing in getting rid of it and I've never regretted it. I'm very happy with the decision I made and I also learned a valuable lesson from the venture; never trust anyone with money.

I do have some fond memories of the shop, however, as it was always such a hive of activity. We were in competition with a temperance bar next door and it was a busy area. I decorated the walls with photos from my rugby days and it was great to reminisce over them with customers.

One of the pictures was of me at Wembley in 1950 chasing after the legendary Brian Bevan, trailing him by just a few yards. People would often look at it and ask if I managed to catch him.

"Of course not," I'd say. "No-one ever caught Brian, not if they were that far behind."

Chapter Twenty

Bevan was the most unlikeliest-looking rugby player I ever saw. He was so thin and so frail but, blimey, could he run. He was one of the fastest wingers there has ever been and he was so light on his feet. There was no sidestep, just a swerve. He simply ran around people as if they were not there and there was no chance of catching him. I tried at Wembley but he just sailed past. I took a flying dive of about five yards at him but missed and went crashing into the hoardings. The surviving footage of the match might be old and grainy but there is a clear audible clang as I go shooting off the screen at that point.

Bevan never scored in that cup final, though, and that was one of his biggest disappointments. There were not many matches when he didn't score but our full-back Frank Bradley did a good job on him that day and took him out. There was another occasion when Frank, who was normally a superb full-back, switched off and bent down to remove a stone or other object from the pitch and Bevan sneaked over in the corner. I remember shouting in disbelief as I saw what was happening. There was none of that at Wembley with Frank, who was a great character, on top form but sadly we still lost.

Another player that gave Bevan a bit of trouble was Leigh's Nebby Cleworth. Somehow Nebby often seemed to get the better of him, despite not being the fastest of wingers. He was simply a strong and committed runner who would charge straight at his opponents. Bevan did admit that he didn't like facing Nebby, but that was only a minor victory for Leigh and hardly made up for the day when he scored an incredible seven tries against us in March 1948. I spent most of that game trying and failing to tackle him. Bevan was a phenomenal player and I am privileged to have played on the same field. I was deeply saddened when he died relatively young, at just 66, and I went to his funeral.

Mr Rugby Leigh

Aside from the rugby, school and shop, I did play one other role in Leigh public life, that of a councillor. I got interested in local politics and decided to stand for the old Leigh Borough Council as a Liberal candidate. I got voted in and served for three years. Again, that was something I really enjoyed. I was one of only two Liberals and with Leigh being such a Labour stronghold we were outvoted on every single issue, but it was still good fun. I might even have considered standing again had I not been offered a position on the board at Leigh RLFC. It was obvious then something had to give. Evelyne put her foot down and told me it was not feasible to sit on both the council and the board while I had so many other work and family commitments. I had to make a choice and rugby league was the clear winner.

*

Chapter Twenty-one

I loved rugby league so much that I knew I wanted to stay in the game in some capacity after I finished playing. Coaching was something that appealed initially and I started making plans to get involved long before I hung up my boots.

I was still playing at Leigh when I signed up for a coaching scheme set up and run by Trevor Foster, the legendary Bradford and Great Britain second row, at Headingley. Trevor was a lovely fella whom I'll never forget. He became a firm friend and was great company. I did really well on the course, which featured an exam at the end. I think being a teacher gave me an advantage over some of the others and I finished with top marks for the actual coaching section and was third overall, good enough for a grade-one pass. Gus Risman, another great player of my era, took the course at the same time and also came through with flying colours. Gus had made his name as an outstanding back for Salford in the 1930s but continued to play with distinction for Workington and Batley after the War in a remarkable career spanning 25 years. He put what he learnt to good use as he went on to coach Salford, Oldham and Bradford. I had one other link to him in that his son Bev, who actually made his name in rugby union, was one of the star players at Leigh when I returned to the club as a director in the 1960s.

I still had some playing years left in me after qualifying as a coach but I continued to plan for a possible future career by helping Trevor run his courses. In subsequent years they were held at Bisham Abbey, which was a terrific place right on the River Thames. We always did it in the summer and we'd often get glorious weather. I remember well lads taking their shirts off and getting burned. They'd then peel terribly when they scrummed down. Trevor and I also ran courses at Otley for schoolchildren during the holidays. They were good fun too. We'd take over a school and sleep in the hall. Sadly, none of these courses are still running.

It was because of this experience that an offer came along from Wigan to coach their A team and assist first-team boss Jim Sullivan. I was still playing at Widnes at the time but it was too good to refuse. Wigan were a huge club with fine players and the opportunity to work with Jim was irresistible. He had been one of the greatest players of all time, a fine full-back and a superb goalkicker. Like Jimmy Ledgard, he could land a ball exactly where he wanted. He was a great judge of a ball and even as a coach he still used to take great delight in hitting the crossbar in training from any angle. That was one of his party pieces. I could not say no.

My role with the first team on matchdays chiefly involved running out with the water but I still enjoyed the experience. Jim's team-talks were remarkable for their brevity and repetition. Before every game he would place a ball on the table and start patting it. "Men," he'd say. "This is a golden egg. As long as you've got it, they can't score. As long as you've got it, you can score." It was the same talk every time but it proved a good motivational tool. He was right too. If you don't have the ball you can't score, it's simple. Possession is nine-tenths of the law in this game.

Running the A team was a challenge, however. It too was enjoyable but it was very trying at times. The pressure to keep on winning was immense. If you started losing you got booted out, there were no two ways about it. I had a good first season but by the second year a lot of my best players had been promoted to the first team and their replacements were not as good. Results took a turn for the worse and I ultimately paid for that with the sack. They only accepted success at Central Park.

Undeterred, I looked around for other coaching opportunities and found one with struggling Liverpool City. Going there proved a big mistake. I lasted for just 12 months because it was such a struggle with no players and no money. A coach is only as good as his team and only a couple of the lads there could do anything. There was no cash to buy people in and you had to rely on the second-rate juniors left after Widnes had signed the best of the kids in the area. The facilities were also dreadful. The ground was just an open field with no stands and a hut for the dressing rooms. It was terrible and after just one year I decided I had had enough. It was a shame the game could never establish itself in Liverpool and I would have loved to have seen the club succeed but when I was there it seemed like a hopeless task. They did try for quite a while at Liverpool City and then Huyton after that but sadly it didn't work.

I never got back into top-line coaching after that. I realised it was not really for me. It's alright when you're winning, but if you start losing there is only one way – out.

It can be a very insecure job and there is no way I would ever have gone into it full-time. I was quite happy teaching for a living and I wouldn't have risked my livelihood by giving that up to coach. I could have carried on doing it part-time somewhere but after my experiences with Wigan and Liverpool City I decided against that too. From then on, as far as coaching was concerned, I decided to stick to school lads. I ran the St Peter's team and coached the Leigh town schoolboys side and I was more than happy doing that. In time I also became president of the Leigh Junior Schools Rugby League and took an active role in their fundraising activities.

Giving up top-level coaching actually paved the way for my return to the Leigh club. I had never stopped watching Leigh's teams, even after they had said they no longer wanted me. I may have gone on to greater things at Widnes and then worked at two other clubs, but I still lived and earned my crust in Leigh. The town was my home and I was still a big Leigh fan at heart. I had no axe to grind despite how I was treated in my later days as a player. It seemed only natural to pop along and watch when I could, whether that be junior or senior teams. I was even there watching Leigh A on the morning of my Challenge Cup semi-final against Bradford. My decision to stop coaching merely gave me the chance to go more often and I soon got involved with the supporters' club again. They welcomed me with open arms and no-one showed any bitterness towards me. Had I been the one that had rejected Leigh to try to find a better club all those years earlier there might have been some animosity, but it was not an issue. It was good to be back.

I was soon appointed president of the supporters' club, which was a great honour. It was a thriving organisation, as I had experienced at close quarters during the building of Hilton Park, and I really enjoyed everything about it. The team were also in reasonable shape on the field with Jimmy Ledgard still going strong before moving back to Dewsbury and the likes of Mick Martyn, Bill Kindon and Walt Tabern to the fore. Sadly it was also a time tinged with tragedy as one of our best lads, the hard-tackling captain and loose forward Peter Foster, was killed in a car crash and chairman James Hilton also died.

It was after the passing of another director, Fred Palmer, a local fishmonger who had been involved in the club since the War, that I was unexpectedly offered a seat on the board in 1962. The circumstances were sad but I gladly accepted. I then spent the following 10 years on the board, witnessing at first hand or being involved in the decisions that led to the club's finest hour – the 1971 Challenge Cup win – and the slump that followed, as well as all the highs and lows that led up to it. It was a tremendous roller-coaster.

I soon immersed myself in everything the club did and I seldom missed games, home or away, whether that be with the seniors, under-21s or colts team. We had board meetings every Tuesday and met again on Thursdays to discuss one of our most important responsibilities, the selection of the first team. This was never something I was comfortable with and thought it was wrong that the board should pick the side. I like to think that I was always fair and objective in my choices but I don't think that was the case with everyone. Other directors often had their favourites and if they'd signed a certain player they'd want to pick him every week regardless of whether he was worth his place or not. That was clearly an unfair system. I argued that the coach should be the man in charge as he knew the players best and would not have any such allegiances. He would always pick the best possible team because it would be in the interests of his job to do so. It was an argument I won and my old friend Gerry Helme became the first coach to be given sole responsibility for selecting the side when he succeeded Alan Prescott in 1963-64.

Obviously I never did any coaching at Leigh myself – they wouldn't have had me anyway – but one area where I did get positively involved in was scouting. I used to travel far and wide looking for potential players and was always taking games in, league and union. A friend of mine, Ken Bruce, who was also the head at the grammar school, often accompanied me on long trips and we once went all the way to Bridgend to watch a player only to discover he was out injured when we got there. That proved a huge wasted journey and to top it off we then had to drive home back up the M6 in thick fog. It was a frightening experience with all the lorries thundering past and it seemed like we barely got out of second gear. There were moments that night when I didn't think we were going to get home.

Trips to Wales were always an adventure. The rugby union clubs were understandably paranoid about scouts from rugby league coming down to look at their players and I usually donned the hat and coat and kept my head down. The accent was sometimes a giveaway so I'd keep quiet after getting a programme. I'd do my best to try to fit in and that's why I'd always take someone like Mr Bruce with me. That made it look a bit less conspicuous. Even so, it still seemed sometimes that they could sniff you out from miles away. You'd be in big trouble if they found out you were from up north and I'd never dare go into a bar after the game. I'd always come straight home.

We weren't the only rugby league club at it though. I once went down to Newport in the hope of signing David Watkins but saw to my frustration, as I surveyed the crowd, the faces of Griff Jenkins and one of the Salford directors. I knew immediately they would be there to watch the same player and that we'd have no chance. Salford of course got their man and Watkins went on to become a legend at The Willows.

I used to comb the local area too and often went to places such as Fylde, St Helens and Tyldesley. Another player I attempted to sign was the future England rugby union coach Brian Ashton, whose father had actually been one of the volunteers that helped build Hilton Park. Brian was playing for Tyldesley and looked a good scrum-half but unfortunately he had no interest in turning professional. He wanted to stick to his rugby union.

That was fair enough, it was a matter of preference. He wanted to play one game above the other. A number of players did switch codes, of course, and that is a trend which continues to this day – only in reverse. Union is where all the money is now and I can't blame anyone for moving across. It is a chance to make a very good living. Shaun Edwards is one of the prime examples. He has done remarkably well as head coach at Wasps and defence coach with Wales. I've no idea what a defence coach is but good luck to him.

It does frustrate me though how much rugby league has to play second fiddle to rugby union in the national media. When I get my paper I usually see two full pages of rugby union and barely any league. It's a shame. We've lost our popularity and I don't know why. In rugby union they do all that hacking to get the ball only to pass it out and kick it to the opposition. That's all the game seems to be sometimes and I don't understand it. Rugby league is a much better spectacle but is not treated equally. I do concede, however, that there is a lot more kicking in our game now than there was in my day. After every six tackles a team usually kicks. There was none of that when I was playing and if you kicked it straight to the opposition in those days the coach would usually go mad.

One man whose services I did manage to acquire, and it

was the greatest thing I ever did for Leigh, was the one and only Alex Murphy. The team had struggled throughout the 1965-66 season, eventually finishing 20th, and the campaign ended with a number of players requesting transfers. Two of the team in Geoff Fletcher and Bev Risman did leave and there was a further blow as crowd favourite Mick Martyn, our prolific tryscoring second row, announced his retirement. Thankfully the numerous requests of the club and fans, as well as a petition signed by every player, persuaded him to give it another year. Nevertheless, the team still needed a shot in the arm and we got it with our audacious signing of Murphy, a coup which stunned the game.

Murphy was only 27 but was already one of the best scrum-halves there had ever been with a medal collection to match. He was like lightning. He was so quick off the mark, so skilful and so strong. He was devastating coming around the blindside and difficult to pin down. He is the best player I have ever seen. The likes of Roger Millward and Tommy Bradshaw were fine half-backs too but Murphy had the edge for me because he was more robust. I would have given my right arm to have played alongside him. The only time I did get on the field with him we were in opposition in a trial match and I didn't enjoy that much. He was just too strong and too good.

In normal circumstances we would not have had a sniff of signing him and even though he had fallen out with St Helens and been transfer-listed for £12,000 it was still highly unlikely. That sort of fee was well beyond our means and that of a lot of other clubs. Yet nothing ventured, nothing gained and with a little lateral thinking I hatched a plot I thought might just have an outside chance of tempting him. Players like Murphy did not become available very often and it was worth a try.

Chapter Twenty-one

I remembered that a few years earlier Wigan had put their fine Kiwi stand-off Cec Mountford on the transfer list for a prohibitive fee. They had hoped that would ward off potential suitors but the move backfired as Warrington came in and offered him a position as a coach. Wigan could do nothing about that as there was nothing to stop a player becoming a coach elsewhere. He still couldn't play, as Wigan retained his registration, but once they realised they had lost him anyway, they could then only ask for a small amount. With this in mind, I told the board we "could do a Cec Mountford" and they agreed it was worth a go.

I put our plan into action one Sunday morning as I went round to his house to speak to him. He wasn't in but his wife Alice came to the door and told me that I'd be able to find him playing golf at Grange Park. I set off immediately to find the course and once I got there I parked up and waited patiently for him to finish his round. When I finally saw him I approached him and asked if he would be interested in coming to Leigh as coach. I explained that we couldn't pay the asking price to take him as a player but Saints could not prevent him coming as a coach. Once he'd done that they would then have to relent and let him go cheaply. They'd rather have something than nothing.

At first he used some rather coarse language to tell me where to go, but I persisted. The more I talked to him the more he began to come round to the idea. He was having a rough time at St Helens and wanted to get away. I urged him to come to see our chairman, Major Jack Rubin, at his offices on Henrietta Street. He agreed and we got him signed up.

There began the greatest period in Leigh's history. Murphy did not play for us until a league embargo was lifted the following year but his influence was evident almost immediately. As well as being a fine player he was also a hugely inspirational figure and a great motivator. We knew with those attributes he had the potential to become a fine coach and we were not mistaken.

*

Chapter Twenty-two

The arrival of Alex Murphy as coach sadly meant that my old mate Gerry Helme was edged out. This wasn't something I was best pleased about as we had been good friends and training partners in our playing days but results were not good. As I knew from personal experience, the coach, while taking the praise when things went well, carried the can when they didn't. The chance to bring in Murphy was too good to miss and Gerry had to be the fall guy. His departure was not immediate as we initially brought Murphy in to work alongside him as a joint coach but that arrangement was not to last. Thankfully I wasn't the one that had to tell Gerry when his services were no longer required, the chairman did that, and at least we managed to remain friends.

I had nothing but admiration for Gerry. He was a great player in his day. Not many players can say they have won the Lance Todd Trophy once, so to become the first to claim it twice marked him out as something special. I cursed him after the first of those, coming at Widnes' expense in 1950, but I was pleased for him when he repeated the feat on one of the game's landmark nights four years later. I was there to see it too, one of the 102,569 who officially crammed into Odsal to watch Warrington's famous replayed final against Halifax. What an occasion that was. The people were like flies everywhere on that steep banking and everyone knows the attendance figure was really much higher. Gerry won the game with a late try. After retiring he remained a great servant to rugby league. Sadly he died young, in his fifties, and that was a big loss to the game.

As awkward as removing Gerry was, it was obvious straightaway things were going to change for the better. Murphy did not dwell on the fact that he couldn't play and quickly set about stamping his authority on the team. He was a huge character in the game and had the respect of the players immediately. No matter how big or small they were he treated them all the same. That cocksure attitude that had served him so well on the field transferred well to the dressing room and the players responded. They hung on his every word and he had them in the palm of his hand.

Murphy was not a great tactician but he was an incredible motivator and knew how to get the best out of players. He did not mince his words and you had to shut the dressing-room door when he was at it, giving the players a rollicking, especially if the team weren't doing so well. There was one occasion when I left the dressing room at half-time and forgot to close the door behind me. The whole corridor were treated to one of his specials. He really let the team have it, giving them both barrels. It was extraordinary but in a funny way it was a treat to hear. Because of the respect he commanded we knew it worked and it was great to see such passion.

Murphy's methods were unconventional but highly effective and his record speaks for itself. In his first five-year spell in charge from 1966-71 Leigh reached five cup finals. Two of them were in the Lancashire Cup – won one, lost one – and two in the Floodlit Trophy – won one, lost one. They alone would have represented remarkable success but then there was the glory of 'Wembleigh '71' at the end of a season in which we finished fourth. Without a doubt, Alex Murphy put Leigh back on the map.

One of the best examples of his off-the-wall approach that I can recall was in his handling of winger Rod Tickle and the continuing problem of his refusal to score as close to the posts as possible. Tickle had all the attributes a winger needed. He was lightning fast, one of the quickest men to have played the game in my opinion, and he could catch pigeons. He could be lethal out wide but the only problem with him was that he always ran in a straight line up and down the touchline. After games you would usually see a line of footmarks where he had been running. He would sometimes run 60 or 70 yards with the ball but when he got to the corner, even if there was no-one near him, he would just put the ball down. He seemed to have no idea where the goalposts were. I think Murphy got sick of telling him about it and after one of his long-range specials at Blackpool one day, when we were winning by a few, he decided enough was enough.

"Get the ball and kick the goal," Murphy shouted to him. Tickle protested and suggested he had never kicked a goal in his life. "Rodney," Murphy said firmly. "Get that ball and kick the goal."

Tickle did as he was told but his attempt barely got halfway to the posts and he was embarrassed. Murphy had made his point in an unusual way but the lesson was finally learnt. After that Tickle always ran to the posts.

When Murphy took over the team had lost 10 of their first 15 games in all competitions in 1966-67 but he sparked a revival that led to us finishing 13th, a position that had seemed most unlikely when he arrived. Things then really kicked on the following season as Murphy pulled on a Leigh shirt for the first time and we reached the final of the BBC2 Floodlit Trophy. We were beaten by Castleford but the semi-final win over Wigan lived long in the memory of many. Another satisfying aspect of the season was the emergence of young prop Dave Chisnall, an excellent signing by Murphy and someone who had caught my eye playing in the amateur game.

We then reached the semi-finals of the Lancashire Cup and the Floodlit Trophy in 1968-69. We lost to St Helens and Wigan respectively but confidence was growing and a defeat by Salford in the November of that campaign proved our last in the league at home for two-and-a-half years.

We made a superb start in 1969-70, reaching the Lancashire Cup final amid a run of 16 wins from 18 games in all competitions. Unfortunately, Swinton pulled off a shock 11-2 win but Murphy promised not to let the fans down again and was as good as his word as the team bounced back to win the Floodlit Trophy after stunning wins over Cas, 12-11 in the semis, and Wigan, 16-11 in the final.

It was Leigh's first trophy for 14 years but the best was still to come with a double success the following season that included the most famous prize in the game. Again, the team started like a house on fire, losing only three times in 21 games and powering to victory in the Lancashire Cup, beating Saints in the final. After that win, in November 1970, Murphy said he felt the team was ready to win a Challenge Cup. His confidence excited everyone and was not misplaced. He was a very positive chap, never negative, and was determined to achieve his goal.

It became possible as wins over Bradford, Widnes, Hull

and Huddersfield, the last a dull, tryless affair, carried us through to Wembley. It was a great adventure. The mighty Leeds were to be our opponents and despite losing only eight of 34 league games all season, we were second favourites by some distance. Yet Murphy, bullish as ever, did not know the meaning of the word defeat and prepared his team perfectly. "The bigger they are, the harder they fall," he said in typically abrasive fashion. "We are going to hit them like a ton of bricks."

We had good training sessions in the build-up and the lads were in a great mood as they went up to the stadium for the traditional walkabout. They were jumping up and down and full of life, like caged tigers waiting for the game. I remember a record being played over the loudspeakers and the great winger Joe Walsh and I did a waltz in the middle of the field. By contrast Leeds, who arrived a little later than us, were a miserable looking lot. There was not a smile amongst them and they had the look of a beaten side even then. Murphy certainly noticed that.

He continued his preparation in the most unorthodox of ways. When I played at Wembley with Widnes we had to be in bed for 10pm on Friday night but Murphy imposed no curfew. He told the lads to go to bed whenever they felt like it. He knew the lads were excited and felt if they turned in early they wouldn't be able to sleep. He said they could stay up as late as they wanted playing cards or dominoes or whatever and should only go to bed when they felt their heads dropping. Not surprisingly some were up until 2am, almost unheard of the night before a Wembley final, but it worked a treat. That was obvious from the moment they walked out for the game. They were really up for it whilst Leeds all still seemed to have their heads down. Murphy again spotted that and said: "Look, they've gone before they've even started, you've got them."

I must admit, I never dreamt we were going to win but Murphy was right. You could see as the game went on that Leeds had no chance. From the beginning to the end, there was only one team in it. Our forwards crushed theirs and in the backs David Eckersley and the Lance Todd Trophy winner, Murphy himself, ran rings round them. Stuart Ferguson was also on top form with his goalkicking and we won convincingly 24-7. It was a wonderful performance and a pleasure to watch; quite a contrast from when I played there.

The one moment of controversy in the game infamously resulted in Syd Hynes becoming the first man sent off in a Wembley final after an off-the-ball headbutt on Murphy. I know it did look like Murphy played it up a little bit as he went off on a stretcher, and came back on later, but I don't think there is any doubt Hynes butted him. There were some stories claiming Murphy winked to someone as he was carried off and I have no idea whether they are true or not but I think the referee got the decision right. I have watched the game several hundred times since and although Hynes goes out of shot as the camera pans across you can see Murphy's head going back at the edge of the screen. The funny thing is, I actually missed the incident at the time because I was following the ball. Yet I made up for that in the weeks and months that followed as I toured the pubs and clubs of Leigh showing the game on cine film. There were no video recorders back then of course and everyone wanted to see the game again. I visited virtually every licensed premises in the town and I reckon I must have known every blade of grass at Wembley by the end of the run.

I've also seen the game on video countless times and I always smile at the BBC commentary of Eddie Waring. He was so biased towards Leeds it was untrue and like many in the media he was probably expecting the Loiners to win easily. The bit that really made me laugh was when one of their players, David Hick, found his way to the line late on only to be denied by a Ferguson tackle. Waring got excited as he willed Hick to score but his voice tailed off dramatically when he realised it was not to be. "Hick's in, Hick's in... in touch," he cried. Whenever I saw Waring after that I always reminded him about it.

The cup win captured the imagination of the town like nothing before or since. I couldn't believe the turnout as we returned home with the trophy on the Sunday. The crowds started as far away from Leigh as Boothstown and went all the way through Astley, Tyldesley and Atherton to the town centre. Estimates reckoned 100,000 people lined the streets and everywhere was bedecked in red and white. I don't think anyone stayed in their house and when we got to the town hall we could hardly move. It had been 50 years since Leigh's previous Challenge Cup success and everyone in the town was determined to enjoy it.

Little did they know the bombshell that was about to hit them.

*

Chapter Twenty-three

The celebrations after the Challenge Cup win went on long and hard, naturally so. After all, it was the greatest moment in the club's history and we had to make the most of it. For me going to Wembley as a player and a director was a double to savour and winning on the second of those occasions was something to remember. The buzz in the town was also unbelievable and as well as touring with the cine film I also took the cup into school to show the children. They were very excited and loved that.

Yet sadly, even as Alex Murphy stood on the balcony at the town hall thanking everyone for their support, the seeds of the club's demise had been sown. To ensure he was cheered rather than booed he didn't mention it then but he had already told us, on the bus back home, that he was leaving us for Warrington. It came like a bolt from the blue, to me anyway, and didn't half take the gloss off the celebrations.

I was absolutely stunned. I just couldn't believe it. As I

looked at the crowds cheering outside the town hall I wondered what they would think if they knew what I did. It was an awkward feeling and when the papers started reporting Warrington's interest the following day the party started to go flat. The move was confirmed later in the week and we tried to ensure continuity by appointing loose forward Peter Smethurst as player-coach.

Losing Murphy was bad enough but that alone did not bother me too much because I knew deep down he was not going to stay with us forever. What really concerned me was the thought that Murphy might want to take a number of our players with him. I made my feelings known to the board immediately and told them we had to act to prevent a raid from Wilderspool. Sadly a lot of what I said fell on deaf ears and my worst fears were confirmed.

When Murphy left our then chairman Jack Harding was quoted in one of the local papers saying: "Apart from selling the ground we could not have increased what was a very handsome offer to keep Alex Murphy at Leigh." He was right there but after that I don't think he did enough to stop Murphy taking our best players with him. In fact, I blame him and the other board members for the whole fiasco that followed. In seemingly no time at all we lost half the pack in Dave Chisnall, Geoff Clarkson and Kevin Ashcroft as Murphy came back to cherry-pick his favourites. I wouldn't have let any of them go and I told Jack that in no uncertain terms but every time the Warrington chairman Ossie Davies asked about a player he seemed to get what he wanted. It was heart-breaking and I couldn't understand it. Warrington had to pay but I argued that we didn't need the money and should be looking to rebuild around those players. It was crackers to get rid of them and I could not make any sense of the madness.

What I did know was that I was getting heaps of hate

mail through my door each day. It was very upsetting for both me and my wife. A lot of the letters were anonymous and most of them angry in tone. People were demanding to know why I had sanctioned the transfers of our best players but the truth was I objected to every single one of them.

Chisnall was the first to go, followed by Clarkson. I was powerless to stop it. I remember Clarkson leaving very well. We had been playing at St Helens the previous day and after the game I noticed Jack Harding chatting to Ossie Davies in the corner of the boardroom. I sensed something untoward might be going on so went over to investigate. I asked what they were talking about and Jack told me Warrington were after Clarkson. I told him firmly that such matters needed to be discussed in the boardroom at Hilton Park, in formal meetings, not over a drink at Knowsley Road. I walked away having made my point but was furious when I picked up a paper the next morning and saw a headline reading 'Clarkson joins Warrington'.

Ashcroft was the next to be tempted by the Wire. He came round to my house to beg to be allowed to leave. I told him clearly that in my opinion it should be out of the question. I said he should be left behind the railings, on the sidelines in other words, until he was ready to play for us again. I told him about all the letters I was receiving but in the end I couldn't do anything to stop him. The board opted to take the cash and overruled me. It was crazy because we were not in any financial trouble at the time, largely due to the cup win, but my opinion counted for little. After that I decided I had had enough and resigned from the board. I couldn't take any more.

The man I felt sorry for the most was Peter Smethurst. I never met a more dedicated or enthusiastic bloke in my life. As a player he always brought his own training kit in a little bag and he'd have it washed and cleaned ready. He was a great example to the rest of the team, very professional in his preparation and always giving 100% on the field. He was a really tough forward and didn't half get through some tackling, especially at Wembley, and had a crooked nose to prove it. He was a very popular figure at the club too, although I'll never forget the time before he joined us when he upset Stan Owen while playing for Swinton in a game at Hilton Park. As play was going on on one side of the field, Smethurst and Owen clashed on the other and the fiery prop comically set off after him. Peter knew Stan had quite a temper and ran away and it was very funny watching him weave his way around the field trying to evade capture as play went on elsewhere. It was like watching two children in the playground.

Away from rugby Peter had a butcher's shop in Swinton and he used to bring us some lovely steaks to board meetings when he was coach. Unfortunately he was on a hiding to nothing trying to succeed Murphy. The team was decimated and he never had a chance from the start, despite his commitment. The board did not give him enough time and he was sacked after just a few months. That was far too soon and he deserved much better than that, although he did get a second short stint about a decade later, again succeeding Murphy. He was a great man and I was very upset when he died young. Much like Gerry Helme, another former Leigh coach and fitness fanatic, he passed away far too prematurely.

Murphy, with our players helping him, built a fine team at Warrington and enhanced his already huge reputation considerably. That was great for him but it was disaster for Leigh and we finished 16th the year after he left. The demise continued and two years after that we were relegated following the introduction of a two-division structure. By then I was just a supporter again. Even though I had walked away from the board after the sales of our best men I could not let the game or the club go. I gave the boardroom a wide berth for quite a while but I carried on going to watch the games.

*

Chapter Twenty-four

Evelyne and I had four children and all of them were very special to us. Sadly two of them are no longer here and their deaths have been among the most difficult things I have ever had to deal with. Nothing can prepare you for losing one of your children. It is one of the toughest things a parent can go through. Our son Trevor was just 25 when he was killed and we never got over it. I miss him every day.

Trevor was the twin brother of Jean and the pair of them came between our first child Fiona and our fourth, Ronnie. I'll never forget the twins' birth – because I missed it. They arrived on February 20, 1949. I was out of the first-team picture at Leigh at the time and had actually been playing in an A team fixture at Oldham. Evelyne was not due for another two months and there was no sign of any waters breaking when I set off for the game as normal. It was only when I got home and was met by my mother-in-law that I learned something was amiss. She told me Evelyne had gone into premature labour and been taken to St Mary's hospital in Manchester. I realised immediately it must be serious because that was a specialist centre. I had been looking forward to my tea but I abandoned that and shot off straightaway. Unfortunately I was too late in getting there, as when I arrived I was told I had already become a father again, to a boy and a girl. They only weighed 4lb each and looked like skinned rabbits but, thankfully, they were both alright and lived.

The baby of the family, Ronnie, was born five years later in Firs Maternity home, just at the side of the school where I worked, and his mother doted on him. Like her, I loved my family immensely and always did my best for them. I never forgot what my childhood was like and was determined my children's would be better. They were never going to experience the horrors my father inflicted upon me and I loved them with all my heart.

I certainly made sure they had good holidays. After falling in love with Italy during the War I was keen to go back as often as I could and show my family all the nice places I had seen. We went a number of times in the summers, driving down in the car. We couldn't afford to stay in hotels so we camped but they were great trips. I knew where the best places to go were and everyone really enjoyed them. It was quite a treat as travelling abroad was a rarity for most families then. In fact, it was so unusual that after one trip Jean was asked to stand up in school assembly and tell the whole school about it.

I took the family all round Italy, to all the great city sights and plenty more interesting places besides, such as the Isle of Capri. We continued to holiday there until well after the kids had grown up. On one occasion Fiona's husband, Terry, accompanied us and was completely caught out by the sun. He was not used to it and was walking around with no top on because it was so hot. I warned him to cover up but it was too late as the next day he couldn't get out of bed because of sunstroke.

My parenting skills weren't always up to scratch, however. When Jean was about four or five I took her to a rugby match at Leigh and managed to leave without her. I didn't even realise I'd forgotten her until I got home and Evelyne asked where she was. That frightened me to death and I raced back immediately. I couldn't believe what I'd done. As I got towards to the ground I could see her from across the road but then she started running towards me. That scared me even more but fortunately I just managed to get across quickly enough and cut her off. She could easily have run into the road and been killed. I was so upset afterwards thinking about what could have happened to her and was very angry with myself. I had been so stupid. I don't know what made me forget her but I made sure I never, ever did it again.

I had the satisfaction of seeing all my children turn out well. Trevor was a great lad. He was brilliant on computers and got a good job operating them at the Daresbury Nuclear Physics Laboratory. They were big old things that used to fill rooms in those days but he could do everything on them. He was also very handy and very practical. He built a garage and an extension for me and his mother and was always doing favours for friends. My love of rugby rubbed off on him too and he became a pretty useful player, although he chose to play only recreationally and union was more his game.

He was very committed to Leigh rugby union club and captained the side. He was always at the club in his spare time, socialising or doing odd jobs, and sometimes it seemed like he was never away from the place. He could have made it in rugby league but he was never interested in going professional. I think he enjoyed the booze and socialising too much for that.

That did not stop Salford trying to sign him once. He caught their eye playing for the Leigh A team after I talked him into making the numbers up. We were two players short and needed him but it was at a time when rugby league and rugby union were really at each other's throats and he was initially reluctant when I asked him. He feared he'd be banned from playing the 15-man game again if he got caught but I assured him he wouldn't. It was a Friday night and there was hardly likely to be many people there. No-one would ever know. His rugby union team played on a Saturday too so there was no clash. He eventually agreed and, typically, had a blinder.

He played on the left wing and scored two cracking tries, racing three-quarters of the length of the field for both. He had plenty of pace. After the game the Salford chairman, Brian Snape, came over to speak to me. He was a very rich man, with money to burn.

"Hey Tommy, is that your lad?" he asked. When I told him it was he asked why I hadn't signed him up. I said I wouldn't sign him for Leigh because, as I was a director of the club, it wouldn't be fair. The directors still picked the team in those days. Yet that was not the only reason. I added that he had passed the age where he wanted to turn pro. He had other things going on in his life and was only filling in because we were short. That did not wash with Mr Snape, who asked if I would mind if he had a word with him anyway. I told him to go for it but warned him he was probably wasting his time.

I was proved right. Mr Snape came back a short while later and confirmed what I already knew; Trevor was not interested. He said he had made a good offer too – and I believed him on that – but still Trevor could not be tempted. That was a pity as I think he would have made a cracking rugby league player. He could probably have done with the money too as he was getting a new house at the time but it was his choice. I had no problem with that at all.

It was not long after that that he was involved in a car crash and died soon after. It was so sudden and really knocked me and his mother for six. At first we thought he had escaped with a broken leg but then he developed an embolism and never recovered. We were devastated.

Trevor was actually driving a friend's Mini when the accident occurred. He had seen his friend loading the car to take his family away on holiday and insisted they did a swap. Trevor had just bought a Ford Capri, which was a bit bigger, and felt he could do his mate a favour by lending it to him. He was only going to need a car that week for getting to and from work and it would be no problem.

Trevor was driving the Mini on those windy roads near Culcheth when someone came round a corner on the wrong side of the road and hit him head on. He was left with a broken leg and was taken to hospital in Warrington. Had it happened today I'm sure he would have survived it but the blood clot developed quickly and in turn caused a blockage to the heart.

At first he had seemed alright. I had visited him and he seemed to be coping but the next day I took a phone call and was told I'd better get back, there had been a relapse. I spent quite some time with him but he seemed stable and I decided to leave later on when Jean arrived. We'd arranged it to make sure we had someone with him all the time. I said goodbye to him and he looked at me as if to say the same. I walked out and made my way to the car park but just as I was about to get into the car Jean came running to me. She was green. She told me I'd better go back straightaway. We ran but by the time we got back he was already dead. He'd died at just 25 and all he'd had was a broken leg. I was in pieces. He was such a lovely lad and hadn't done anything to anyone. There is no justice in this world.

Trevor's funeral was one of my saddest days, yet also one of my proudest. The church was packed to capacity. I couldn't believe the number of friends he had made in his short life. I was certainly a very proud dad that day. Trevor left a wife and a young daughter, Cheryl, and I often wonder what he would have been doing now.

*

Chapter Twenty-five

I watched with incredulity as Leigh's Wembley-winning side was dismantled and the club went into decline. It was not all doom and gloom as Les Pearce, having taken over from Peter Smethurst's short-lived successor Derek Hurt, guided the team to victory in the BBC2 Floodlit Trophy in December 1972, but that merely masked the problems. Things steadily went downhill after that. A succession of other coaches came and went, but none could arrest the slide, and it was the best part of a decade before we were back at the sharp end again. Eddie Cheetham, Kevin Ashcroft, Bill Kindon, John Mantle and Tom Grainey all failed to fill the considerable shoes of Alex Murphy. The club were relegated in 1974 and although they were promoted two years later, it was back to Division Two in 1977.

In the end it took something special to stop the rot. Watching Leigh had become a frustrating experience but then the emergence of two homegrown talents and future club legends in John Woods and Des Drummond gave everybody cause for excitement. The pair were outstanding as Leigh romped to the Second Division title in 1978 and optimism again abounded. The team then did enough to avoid the drop the following year and things really kicked on when Brian Bowman, having taken over as chairman, managed to secure the return of Murphy as manager midway through the 1980-81 season.

That gave the club an incredible lift and the players responded once again. Murphy clearly had the magic touch and in seemingly no time at all Leigh were back at the top end of the game. We claimed the Lancashire Cup in September 1981 and sensationally followed that up by winning the league championship for the first, and so far only, time seven months later. It was an unforgettable campaign. There were some fine players in that team and Murphy, the motivational master, in tandem with coach Colin Clarke, organised them superbly.

They were also given tremendous support from the top. Brian, who is a very good friend of mine, was an excellent chairman and took on a job I would never have considered with great relish. His enthusiasm for the game and the club was infectious and that filtered down to the team, spurring them on to great things.

On the field, Woods was the chief inspiration. He was an amazing player who had it all. Not many players have every attribute, but he did. He didn't just punish opponents with his kicking like Jim Sullivan or Jimmy Ledgard, or by simply scoring tries like Billy Boston. He did everything. He could score wonderful tries, kick goals from all angles and tackle like the toughest of forwards. He was a magnificent stand-off, the best Leigh have ever had, and he should have gone on to become one of the game's true greats. His only problem was that he couldn't motivate himself for training, but such was his talent he could get away with that. He was such a natural athlete with great speed off the mark and a devastating sidestep. He would find the smallest gaps and be away, in the clear, with few able to catch him. And with all that he was such a nice character. He kept his feet on the ground and away from the game was just a normal bloke.

There were some other excellent players in that team such as Steve Donlan, Phil Fox, Alf Wilkinson and Ray Tabern but, for me, the other stand-out performer was Drummond. Des was a real flyer with a beautiful running style. He was very, very quick and so exciting to watch. Yet what set him apart from other wingers was his strength. He wasn't a very big fella but, by gosh, he was tough. When he hit someone they knew about it and I wouldn't have liked him tackling me. He could really rough players up and his tackles, often executed with perfect timing, were almost as crucial as his tries, of which he scored 16 that season. I remember him excelling in the TV programme *Superstars* and he also did well once in the Powderhall Sprint, the famous handicapped race held in Edinburgh at New Year.

It was under Brian that I got involved with the club again. After retiring as a headmaster in 1982 I suddenly found I had a huge void in my life and needed something to keep my brain ticking over. I had always lived a busy life and the loss of routine left a feeling of emptiness I needed to fill. The lack of stimulus was mind-numbing and I don't think it is an exaggeration to suggest it could have killed me. I was itching to get out of the house more often and so, urged by my wife, I offered to help the club out in any way I could. They were very receptive and gave me some work helping in the office as assistant secretary. That gave me just the lift I needed and I've been working for the club ever since. I have a little desk and I go in every morning and do jobs such as filling in the statistics from games and answering the phone.

Sadly, the fairytale return of Murphy was not to last as Wigan came in with an offer for him that he couldn't refuse and he decamped to Central Park. Without his influence we slipped away from the lofty heights and the halcyon days have never been revisited. Murphy did briefly come back twice more but we became something of a yo-yo club, flitting between the two divisions for a while before being relegated again in 1994 and then sitting outside of the top flight for more than a decade.

Depressingly, the club got into serious financial difficulties a number of times in that period and we very nearly went out of business altogether. The first crisis came after Keith Bell and Ian Hart, two prominent directors, overstretched themselves by paying out extraordinary money for ordinary players in the late 1980s. The signing of David Stephenson from Leeds for a record fee was a particular disaster as he hardly ever played. We ended up with a debt of around £350,000 and went into liquidation.

Thankfully, the support of the public kept us going just long enough for an 11th-hour rescue bid to come in from an Irishman called Tim Maloney. The public responded brilliantly to our pleas for help and raised quite a lot of money but it was still touch and go until Tim, thanks to good work by Tony Cottrell, agreed to step in. The deadline had been looming large and had he not come on board then, the club might easily have gone out of existence.

Tim was a funny bloke but he did some good for the club. He bought out the players' contracts and shored things up for a couple of years. Another good thing he did was to rid the boardroom of all the freeloaders that used to pile in there on matchdays. There was one little gang that came to every game and seemed to spend most of their time propping up the free bar. They didn't show the slightest bit of interest in the rugby and sometimes they didn't even have the decency to go back to their seats for the second half. The number of pints they used to knock back was ridiculous and it was costing the club a fortune until Tim put his foot down in dramatic fashion. When he saw what was going on one afternoon he immediately ordered the bar to close and told them, very publicly, to get out. That was the last we saw of them.

Unfortunately Tim's efforts merely contained our financial problems. We continued to pay out contracts we couldn't afford and it was not long before we were in administration again. This time we were rescued by Mick Higgins and Allan Rowley, who came in and worked hard to get the debts paid off, and a vital ground-sharing agreement with non-league football club Horwich RMI. Until Horwich stepped in, we had feared Hilton Park might have to be sold for houses. Horwich heard of our troubles and sensed an opportunity to acquire a bigger ground. Not put off by the prospect of a six-mile move, they sold off their Grundy Hill home and bought Hilton Park from the administrators. They then rebranded themselves as Leigh RMI and allowed us to share the facilities. It was a move they hoped would allow them to grow and eventually climb to Conference or even Football League level. Based in a town the size of Leigh that seemed a plausible ambition and they did kick on to reach the Conference in 2000, but they have since fallen back again. They renamed themselves Leigh Genesis in 2008 to reflect their new beginnings at Leigh Sports Village.

For us that whole episode was a very close shave, one of many I have experienced over the years. I can certainly say that I have seen the club go through thick and thin. Even in my early days on the board there were times when finances dipped to a perilously low level. Such times have always scared me because I love the club so much and would hate to see it go under. On one occasion I even put the deeds of my house up for collateral to try to help sustain the club through a particularly difficult period. I never told my wife about that – she'd have killed me! – and for a short while I was terrified because I very nearly lost it. I was so relieved when the crisis ended and it was released from the bank.

The mid-nineties rescue put the club on a firmer financial footing, even though performances plumbed the depths in the immediate aftermath. The worst of them was our infamous 94-4 thrashing at Workington in a cup tie in 1995, a game which still makes many connected to the club shudder. It was absolutely horrendous, one of the bleakest days in the club's history. Every time Workington got to the tryline and scored, we'd kick the ball back to them and they'd come and score again. That carried on all through the game and was quite ridiculous. It was like having 13 dead ducks on the field. It was so embarrassing Mick Higgins, who had taken up the role of chairman following his arrival, later ordered all the players to hand in their club blazers.

By the time rugby league switched to summer seasons in 1996 we were playing in the third tier. We managed to get promoted from that division that year, despite finishing third, but the toils continued. Still, I could not knock the enthusiasm of the people upstairs, particularly Allan Rowley.

Allan, the current chief executive and a proud Leyther, has had a long association with the club stretching back to his days on the terraces as a child. I remember coaching him as a schoolboy in the town team before we signed him for the club as a highly promising 20-year-old. He proved himself the most committed of men, never giving less than 100% on the field. He had a few good years with us before moving on to do a job for Workington. He also had spells with St Helens and Swinton before hanging up his boots and I'm sure he gave them everything too. His wholehearted attitude is still evident today and his efforts since coming back at boardroom level have been tremendous. He did have a spell away from the club some time after the mid-nineties rescue, but he is firmly back on board now and continues to serve the club well.

If Allan did have a flaw as a player, though, it was that he listened too much to the folk on the terraces. When he went into a heavy tackle and someone in the crowd shouted out something like, "Stick one on him Allan," he would oblige. He was notorious for it and got sent off a number of times – although, fair play to him, he would take them on big or small.

There is a funny side to Allan too and he has a terrific sense of humour. I know this only too well. These days he has found a niche as the MC at after-game functions but during his playing career he was a notorious practical joker. He was always playing tricks or trying to wind people up. He was the life and soul of any party but one day all his larking about almost caught up with him with serious consequences. I was counting out the players' wages – one of my regular jobs in those days, when we still paid out in cash – and Allan seemed determined to distract me. Wearing nothing but a towel after a session in the gym, he came into the room pleading for help because he thought he was having a heart attack. One of his tricks was the last thing I needed as I was trying to concentrate and, irritated, I bluntly sent him on his way. That was almost a bad mistake as, moments later, Allan collapsed in the corridor. Realising something really was wrong I rushed to my feet but I had little idea what to do. I called for an ambulance and asked the operator for advice. By this stage Allan's towel had fallen off and he was lying completely naked. I was told that I should put him in the recovery position but if he stopped breathing give him the kiss of life. My reaction to that was one of instant shock. "Recovery position? Kiss of life?" I shouted. "He's 16 stone and naked! I'm not kissing him. What if someone comes in?" Fortunately Allan was fine and when I turned 90 there was no better man to have on the microphone at my party than him.

Mick Higgins had his detractors but he also did plenty of good for the club, even though he all but sacked me after he came in. He told me there was no more money to carry on paying me for my job, although I was welcome to continue on a voluntary basis. I just accepted that and carried on.

By this time the club had added Centurions to its name, which was not something I was particularly in favour of. It was done at a time when all clubs were adding new names such as Bulls, Vikings or Warriors but it still seemed unnecessary to me. We'd previously tried calling ourselves the Bears but that didn't last. I've got used to it now but I have two blazers with the borough badge on and two with Centurions on and I know which ones I prefer. Nicknames are nothing new for Leigh though. I remember before the War when the club picked up the unfortunate tag of 'The Comics' after a few lean seasons. It became quite widespread and stuck for a while before eventually dying out.

The best thing Mick Higgins did for Leigh in his few years at the helm was to bring in Ian Millward as coach. That was an inspired appointment and sparked a revival of the club. Millward transformed a struggling side into challengers for promotion and we enjoyed a great season in 1999. We came into the new millennium with genuine hope of pushing for a place in Super League but sadly Millward had already proved too much of a success by then and was tempted by an offer to replace Ellery Hanley at St Helens. It was no surprise to me that he went on to great success at Knowsley Road. We found a good replacement for him in

Paul Terzis but unfortunately his four seasons in charge were characterised by a number of near-misses as we became the bridesmaids of the second-tier competition.

It was not until 2004 that we finally fulfilled our dream of winning a place in Super League. By this time the coach was Darren Abram. I didn't warm to Darren as much as his predecessors but I cannot knock his achievements that year. It was a memorable campaign, full of excitement. Fans still remind me of the moment when I got carried away with it all after our win at Batley on the final afternoon of the regular season. After winning 29-22 at Mount Pleasant to secure top spot in National League One on points difference from Whitehaven, the players celebrated on the pitch. I wanted to be out there with them and rushed down from the stand. I ran out onto the pitch and then caught sight of our magnificent supporters, who were in full voice at the top end of the ground. I charged up the slope towards them and, overcome in the fervour, jumped headlong in the way I might have dived for the tryline some 60 years earlier. It was a crazy few seconds and the crowd went absolutely mad. I admit I forgot just how old I was in the adrenaline rush. My son Ronnie told me later his heart was in his mouth as he saw his 86-year-old father performing a swan dive and I think a few others were worried. But they needn't have been; I was fine – and very happy. It is not every day Leigh win a championship!

Things then got even better as we went on to beat Whitehaven after extra time to win the Grand Final and reclaim a place among the elite. That was a moment to savour, even though we were soon brought down to earth. Super League was just a different kettle of fish altogether, a totally different level, and we were just not ready. All the excitement soon dissipated and the season became a bit of a waste of time. We got licked every week and there was little to enjoy. It was all too predictable as well. Winning promotion was exciting enough but I warned people even then that the team wouldn't be good enough for Super League. We had to get new players in but we didn't have enough time or money. We were out of our depth and it was painful to watch.

Money has long been our problem. All too often in recent years we have lost good players, many of them local lads, to other teams because we can't compete with the contracts they are offering. We have to be cautious but whilst that is sensible, it is frustrating to see so many Leigh lads doing well elsewhere. If we could ever get a lot of those players back I know we'd have a very good team, but we'd never be able to afford it.

Not surprisingly our Super League adventure lasted just one year and not long after that they did away with automatic promotion and relegation. Now we find ourselves back among the chasing pack having not only to build a decent team but fulfil a whole host of other criteria to have a chance of getting back into Super League. I think it is a bit of a shame they have brought in this licensing system. I liked the old days when they only had one league but when they split it into two divisions for practical reasons they struck on a system that worked well. With two going down and two coming up there was always incentive for teams at the bottom and top of each division. I don't know why it couldn't be left like that. It seems the authorities are always meddling and changing the rules and I think the situation we have now is ridiculous.

*

Chapter Twenty-six

Of all the jobs I have done for Leigh, the one that has given me the most satisfaction and enjoyment in recent times has been the one that I am now best known for, timekeeping. I was asked if I would take over the role of timekeeper after the sad passing of the previous incumbent, Jim Hope, who had been a strong supporter of the club for many years. I gladly accepted and have now been doing the job for quite a while. It is an excellent way of keeping involved in the game and I love it.

It is no easy task, though. It requires a lot of concentration as people are always shouting at you, asking how long is left. I just have to ignore them and keep a close eye on the play and, particularly, the referee. If you miss him signalling time off you could be in trouble. I always have two watches on the go, just in case I press the wrong button, and my son Ronnie often accompanies me to help record the stats.

There are always two timekeepers, one from each team.

This is to make sure nothing untoward goes on and there can be no accusations of cheating. So, in theory, I should never be able to get away with blowing the hooter after 75 minutes if Leigh are winning narrowly, although I did once – on one very embarrassing occasion. It was during a game against Bradford when I was working alongside Trevor Foster, a great man with whom I went way back. With Leigh in front with just a few minutes to go I jokingly said to him, "Come on Trevor, press the button. That's time." I laughed and then put my finger on the button. "If you don't press it I will," I teased. I was only jesting and obviously had no intention of really pressing the button until time was up but it was so sensitive that it set the hooter off. My heart skipped a beat, I couldn't believe it. It was a horrendous gaffe.

There was no way of correcting it and the referee had no choice but to blow the final whistle. I felt terrible about it, particularly as the crowd gave Trevor some awful stick as we walked back past them. "Oi Foster, can't you tell the time?" they were shouting. I felt so guilty and apologised profusely to Trevor and thankfully he was great about it. Anyone else might have clocked me one, but not him. I was so lucky it was Trevor and no-one else because he handled it, like he did everything, with such dignity. He told me not to worry and really tried to ease my anxiety. He was a great friend over many years and I was very sad when he died in 2005. We had been together at a game, reminiscing, just weeks earlier. It was early on in Leigh's single season in Super League and I walked back across the field with him after the match. He put his arm around me and said, "We've had some great times haven't we Saley?" He was absolutely right, of course, but sadly I never saw him again after that day.

All I have ever tried to do in my life is enjoy myself and the amount of accolades I have accumulated in later life never ceases to astound me. I was deeply honoured to be made life president of Leigh and the recognition I get from elsewhere in the game and in the wider community is staggering. I am really amazed sometimes at where it all comes from.

One of the most prominent was being awarded the Freedom of the Borough of Wigan, of which Leigh is a part, in 2000. That was a very proud day in my life and the award is something I cherish enormously. It is the highest honour that our councillors can bestow and is quite rare. It was a lovely surprise. I was one of 10 to receive it at the turn of the millennium and there have only been a few more since. As the jurisdiction of Greater Manchester and the Wigan borough is quite modern, it does not confer any ancient privileges such as allowing me to graze sheep in the centre of town or anything like that, but it is something that will stand for time immemorial. Someone did try to convince me that I can now park in the middle of the street and urinate on my offside front tyre with impunity should I wish, but I've no idea where that myth comes from. I certainly don't remember it being mentioned at the ceremony, so I don't think I'll try it!

I was also taken aback when the Rugby Football League inducted me on their Roll of Honour in 2004. I was presented with a special memento to mark the honour by my old pal and Widnes team-mate Colin Hutton, now the Hull KR president, on the pitch at half-time during the Arriva Trains Cup final between our two teams at Spotland. The Roll of Honour was only introduced in 2003, with former Widnes and Great Britain captain Frank Myler the first inductee, so to be in such esteemed company was very special.

In 2008 I received the Merit Award from the Rugby League Writers' Association at their annual dinner. I thought I had gone there for a night out and was quietly enjoying myself when suddenly one of the speakers started talking about me. I couldn't believe it when I was called up to collect the award for services to rugby league. I followed in the recent footsteps of luminaries such as Colin Hutton and the long-serving Salford chairman John Wilkinson in receiving that award and again I was touched.

Leigh completely caught me off-guard when they renamed the Supporters' Club Stand at Hilton Park after me in 2003. How they managed to keep it secret I'll never know. They hid the whole thing really well and I was completely unsuspecting when I arrived at the ground ahead of what I thought was a normal game. I was asked if I would do the team the honour of leading them out to mark my 85th birthday and of course I accepted, but I had no idea what was to come when I walked out onto the pitch. My mouth fell open as I looked up and saw the huge sign above what was now being proclaimed as the 'Tommy Sale Stand'. That really meant a lot to me because I know the effort that went into building that stand. It had its design faults but the supporters' club worked tirelessly to raise money for its construction. They had collection boxes in every pub and club in town and ran dances.

Times were certainly different then. I don't consider it safe to go up Leigh at night now and a lot of towns are the same. There's a lot of drunken rowdiness and it's terrible. Back then various venues held dances that were very enjoyable. I remember a time when there were four places you could go for a dance on Saturday nights; St Joseph's, Leigh Co-op, Henrietta Street Church of England school and Pennington C of E school. Unfortunately they all closed down when fights at the end of the night started to become more common.

Of course the Tommy Sale Stand, like the rest of Hilton Park, is sadly no more after it was bulldozed early in 2009. They invited me back to see it knocked down. In its place I have been granted something even more extraordinary; the naming of a whole road after me. To me it just seems incredible that the street leading up to the lovely new Leigh Sports Village has been named Sale Way. I really don't know what I do to deserve these things. It goes all the way around the ground and whenever someone writes to the club they put Sale Way on the address. It will still be there after I've gone and I struggle to take that in sometimes.

I had been under the impression that Wigan council had decided never to name streets after personalities again after a previous bad experience but they must have changed their mind at some point. We had a really nice ceremony on the day the road was officially named and I treasure the photographs taken of myself and my family beside the Sale Way sign. Two other roads on the complex were also named after Leigh sporting legends. There is Ledgard Avenue, named after our great full-back Jimmy, and Turner Way, after the athlete Geoff. Sadly Jimmy died soon after they named his road and his wife Betty also passed away before the opening of the new stadium, which she was so keen to see. Their daughter and her husband did come and I hope they found it a fitting tribute to a great man.

I must admit I knew little of Geoff Turner, whose road, fittingly, is now the address of Leigh Harriers. He was a high jumper who represented Great Britain at the 1928 Olympics in Amsterdam. I think I vaguely remember him because he was friendly with a butcher I knew.

People have said the road should really be called Tommy Sale Way and I'm told our MP Andy Burnham, who at the time of writing is also the Secretary of State for Health, is on the case. I don't think they'll ever change it though, and it isn't necessary. It's my health I want more than anything and as long as I have that I'm happy. I just wish my wife and the other members of my family that are no longer with us were here as well.

*

Chapter Twenty-seven

One thing I cannot overstate is the importance of the role played by my family throughout my life. They have always been a great, loving support and been with me through all the ups and downs that I have experienced. Evelyne was a wonderful wife and a great mother. She had no interest in rugby, hardly ever came to watch me play and in later years I think she hated the Leigh club for the amount of time I used to spend there. Yet she was always very supportive and on one of the few occasions she did come to see me in action, at Wembley, I know she was very proud.

Her main interests were the house and the children. As long as she had them she was happy. Everything in my house is her doing. All the furniture and all the pictures are where she wanted them and I want to keep things as she had them. The only area in which I'm failing is keeping the kitchen table clear. It's always cluttered, usually with Leigh programmes, and she would not have liked that one bit!

I've been very lonely since she died in December 2006

and miss her so much. I'll admit there were times when I thought she was a nuisance, but I wish she was here causing a nuisance now. I look at where she used to sit sometimes and think I can see her, only for the image to fade away. She was very active until her later years but she died in a home after having two strokes. She lost all her dignity and had to have everything done for her. I couldn't manage her but I went to visit her every day and found it heartbreaking. She didn't like the feeling of helplessness and used to say things like, "Tom, let me die". She prayed every day to die and, very sadly, she did eventually.

That happened just a couple of weeks before Christmas and was the start of a very bad period for our family. A week later Evelyne's sister died and soon after my daughter Fiona discovered she had cancer of the ovaries. She died because of a brain tumour four months later. She was only 67 and it was almost too much to take.

Fiona was a strong woman who had also had some difficult times. She was a devoted mother and for 42 years looked after her severely handicapped son, Simon, unfalteringly. That was hard work because he had to be carried about and she and her wonderful husband Terry had to do everything for him. Sadly Simon also passed away young and Fiona was devastated. I think all that might possibly have taken its toll and shortened her life. She left another son, Julian, and two grandchildren, Finlay and Lucy.

The only aspect of their deaths I can be thankful for is the order they happened. I'm glad Evelyne went before Fiona. The death of Trevor really cut her up and to have seen Fiona go as well would have been unbearable. The two had always been incredibly close, probably because I was away for the first four years of Fiona's life. During that time they developed a special bond that was never broken.

I can't describe the emptiness their losses have left. I

sometimes wonder if it is not true, that am I dreaming and I will soon wake up and see them again. But it is true. I know they are gone forever. Sadly that is life. It has its ups and downs and you have got to take them both.

Thankfully I have still got two good kids left in Jean and Ronnie and I have had the pleasure of seeing them both enjoy good careers. Jean is an audiologist in Leigh and is responsible for my hearing aids. She's warned me not to break them, though. They cost £350 each! She's so good to me and is always popping round to check on me. It's like having a butler sometimes. She goes up and down the stairs and lays clothes out for me each day. I don't know where I would be without her. She is my rock.

Ronnie is an accountant at Southport hospital. He's done very well for himself and I've got the certificate from when he passed his accountancy exams on my wall. He worked really hard for that, studying away in our front room night after night for three solid years. He hardly ever went out but it was worth it in the end. He's often round too and we regularly go out together.

Both have had children of their own and Jean's son James has in turn had two daughters, Skye and Brooke. Ronnie has had three boys; Matthew, David and Stefan. They're all great lads and can often be found at the Leigh rugby union club, where they all play.

I'm still here and still enjoying myself, although I have had a few health scares. One of them was at Liverpool airport ahead of a training trip to Spain with Leigh a couple of years ago. I had just been given a pump for my angina and was told if I had any problems to squirt it under the tongue. I felt I was struggling after the long walk from the bus stop to the check-in desk and so sprayed into my mouth three times. The next thing I was on the deck, passed out. Someone called an ambulance and a doctor and when I came round they asked what I had been using. I told them I'd used my pump three times and that immediately set alarm bells ringing. They told me I should only have used it once because it lowers the blood pressure. Mine had dropped to a level that could have killed me. Not surprisingly, they wanted to take me into hospital for observation but I insisted I was still getting on that plane. Apart from the War, I had never been abroad with a rugby team and I really wanted to go. So, against the advice, I went and we had a very good week. I'm pleased I was able to make it because I'm not sure if I'll be able to go overseas with Leigh again. I was due to go to Toulouse for our 2009 Championship fixture but I realised a few weeks beforehand that I really was not fit enough and pulled out. It is not like me to miss a game but I didn't want to be a burden to the others travelling. It was kind enough for the club to invite me and I was looking forward to it but it could have been a struggle, particularly if there were any long distances to walk. I've got to play safe now. I did at least make it to Wembley for the Challenge Cup final in August. I go every year and hope to continue.

But I also have a lot of trouble with my back and am in severe pain much of the time. Three of the discs have been displaced and are pressing on the nerve. It also affects my left leg and makes me terribly uncomfortable. I should have had an operation to realign the discs in 2008 but, fortunately as it turned out, it never happened. I was actually on the trolley on my way into the theatre when a message came through from the doctor to turn back and see him. He said the operation could not go ahead because I had been taking aspirin. I should have been told to stop at least two weeks beforehand because it thins the blood. They couldn't risk it and so I was rescheduled for a few weeks later. By then, however, I had a chest infection and again they said they were unwilling to perform the surgery. I had to wait again but at my next pre-operation assessment I was told the whole thing was too dangerous. Because of my age, angina and chest complaint there was a serious possibility they could lose me on the table. They said they'd go ahead if I really insisted but I agreed it was just not worth it. I decided I'd rather live with the pain than kick the bucket. It is agony at times, and the seats at rugby grounds are no good for it at all, but I'll put up with it in exchange for living a bit longer. I was cursing aspirin for a while but perhaps it saved my life.

The only time I am free of pain is when I am lying down and most nights I am really glad to get to bed. I'm sure the reason for it is all the rugby I played in my youth. Unfortunately I can't take pain-killers for it because they knock me dizzy. I'm hoping a visit to a pain clinic can help.

In recent years I have also had a prostate operation. That was a frightening experience. I was scared after discovering I couldn't pass water and the doctors sent me straight off to hospital. Fortunately that operation went well. I have also had to have two little growths, one on my nose and one near my eye, removed because they were cancerous. I went to Christie's in Manchester for that. They gave me a little tube with a wire and put me next to a machine. I had to hold it over them for five minutes while they switched it on. After that I was told not to touch them under any circumstances and a week later they dropped off.

So, when people say to me I don't look 91 I say I certainly feel like it. I've had it rough at times but I'm still going and plan to be here for a while yet. I cannot grumble about anything and am reminded most days now how lucky I have been in life when I pop in to speak to people at the new day care centre at Leigh Sports Village. There are people there, young and old, who require a lot of attention and it makes me realise how fortunate I am. I chat to them about all sorts of things, but mostly rugby. Sadly a lot of them don't get to the games so I tell them everything that happened.

I'm fortunate to still be able to get around too because my driving licence was recently renewed for three more years. My car is my legs and I'd hate to be without it. I'm still enjoying life and I'm very happy living in Leigh. I wouldn't move if I won the lottery. My advice to anyone who wants to live a long life is don't retire. Find an activity that is not stressful and keep going. I'm very lucky to have ended up how I have but, as I have mentioned, I have had a good family behind me and I wouldn't have made it without them.

*

Chapter Twenty-eight

Leigh, like Widnes, returned to what was then called the National League in 2006 in the hope of putting together a side capable of challenging for promotion back to the top. Unfortunately Hull KR got their act together a lot sooner and it was they that were elevated to Super League that year. The following season relegated Castleford proved far too strong for the rest of the competition and after that the authorities introduced the licensing system. Now Super League places are renewed every three years based not only on playing strength but a range of criteria. With the move to Leigh Sports Village in mind, we put together a strong application for the 2009-12 period but lost out to Salford and Celtic Crusaders.

That was a body blow to the club and things then appeared to take another turn for the worse in 2009 as a dismal season on the field, in what is now called the Championship, ended in relegation. Fortunately we earned a reprieve a few weeks later as financial problems at Gateshead led to them being demoted instead. That was an unexpected but very welcome development and hopefully, having resigned ourselves to a season in the third tier, the let-off will serve as a wake-up call and provide the spark we need to get the club moving at Leigh Sports Village. Personally, I was not too despondent about relegation because I felt it might offer us the chance to regroup, start winning matches regularly and get the crowd excited about coming to games after a subdued first season at the new stadium. Now there is even greater reason for optimism and with Ian Millward returning as coach I am very excited about 2010.

A lot of the ingredients are in place for a bright future. Firstly, there is no doubt we now have a ground good enough to grace Super League. LSV is a superb facility and it is great to see the team playing in such modern and aesthetically pleasing surroundings. It is far more sophisticated than Hilton Park was. It really is in a different league and seems to have everything. I couldn't believe it when I saw the size of the dressing rooms. They're huge – almost big enough to play matches in. Times have certainly moved on since my day. Showers have replaced the big old communal bath which everyone used to pile into. I actually used to enjoy the craic and a good long soak in them but there's no doubt it's a lot more hygienic now. The water in those baths got dirty in no time, especially the one at our dreadful old Charles Street ground where we used to come off the field caked in mud.

LSV is not only a rugby ground either. It is something for the whole community. There's a classroom full of computers on site which children from local schools come to work in every day and part of the stadium is used as a day care centre for the elderly. There's also a hotel on the complex and the whole thing really is quite an impressive-looking set-up.

I was very proud to be asked to kick off ahead of the first game at the ground, a friendly against Salford in December 2008. They said I'd kicked the first ball at Hilton Park and felt it would be fitting if I did so again at LSV, in addition to the fact I was also club president. I said I'd be honoured, even though I probably hadn't kicked a ball in 40-odd years. When I got to the ground I felt I'd better have a practice and so had a look for a ball. Could I find one? No. What a great start to life in a new stadium, we didn't even have a spare ball! I ended up going out onto the field before the game completely unprepared and I think that showed in my kick!

The new ground was officially opened by the Queen in May 2009. That was another great occasion for the club. Bad weather initially threatened to spoil the day but it cleared up before Her Majesty arrived and it was nice and sunny for her tour of the stadium. The stand behind one of the goals was full of children from local schools and they gave her a great reception. There were also games of tag rugby going on all over the field and I think we gave a good impression of ourselves. After that we went inside for lunch and, along with other club officials, I was introduced to the Queen and the Duke of Edinburgh. Prince Philip even spared a moment to speak to me. Politely addressing me as "young man", he asked what I did at the club and, naturally, I replied with the first thing that came into my head. "I'm the timekeeper," I said proudly. Our chairman Arthur Thomas, who was standing next to me, couldn't believe his ears and nudged me as soon as the prince had gone. "You idiot," he said. "You're the president of the club!"

I am, of course, privileged to be the president of Leigh but that doesn't always cut a lot of ice around Leigh Sports Village. The problem with LSV, for all its functionality, is that we are only lodgers there. The club used to own Hilton Park but the new place is run by a separate management company and we must pay to use it. The first indication I got that things were going to be different was when I was stopped from walking across the pitch by a steward. Going over the field was something I used to take for granted at Hilton Park. I used to do it all the time but when I tried to do it at LSV I was told I would have to walk all the way round. I told him I was the president of the club but that probably wouldn't have made any difference if someone else hadn't intervened and said it was okay. That incident saddened me a little and unfortunately there were quite a few more that have caused me to become a bit disillusioned with the whole stadium move during 2009.

As impressive as the place is, it is just not Hilton Park. It is not as friendly and I don't like some aspects of the new system. I used to walk into the offices at our old home and speak to everybody. At LSV, we are only tenants and some of the camaraderie we used to have has gone. We are told where we can and can't go by the management company's officials and I feel we have lost a little of our identity because of that. At times last year it seemed as if we were not Leigh Rugby League Football Club anymore. James Hilton would have been turning in his grave if he could have seen it.

I'm also worried the club won't be able to afford to stay there in the long term, and where that would leave us I have no idea. We have to pay rent for every room we use and if we don't have a winning team to get decent crowds in we're going to struggle to sustain it. It surely cannot be in the best interests of the people running the complex not to have the town's rugby league team playing there but I can foresee problems if things carry on as they were in our first year at LSV. Leigh Genesis had huge difficulties and I'm worried also that Leigh East, the amateur rugby league club, can't afford to rent the smaller ground built for them next door either. They're being charged too much for a club that is run by volunteers and provides an important community service. At least they're still selling beer at their own prices. At first the LSV company, who charge top whack for a pint at the main stadium, were alarmed when they realised people were flocking to Leigh East's clubhouse on Centurions matchdays to get one cheaper. They tried to force them to put their prices up but the club, with legal backing, stood their ground and they seem to have backed off for now. Leigh East have carried on selling cheaper ale and I hope the people in charge of the stadium take heed.

At least at the Centurions we no longer have to worry about the costs of utilities and phone calls. All bills such as those are included in our rent and that is a bonus, but what you gain on the roundabouts you lose on the swings. The only money the club makes comes from gate receipts – and unfortunately they were not as high as we anticipated in 2009.

The chief reason for that was the poor form of the team. The move was supposed to herald a bright new dawn but without a winning side to generate excitement, it became a bit of a damp squib. You can have the greatest arena in the world but if the side is losing people are not going to come through the turnstiles in big numbers. It's a shame the ground was often less than half-full and that, when added to all the other problems, made for a pretty dispiriting first season there.

One of the first casualties of our underwhelming campaign was the new club shop. O'Neills, the company that were running it, found that it just wasn't viable and closed it down midway through the season. With small crowds and no success to excite the fans, they simply couldn't shift enough shirts or other merchandise to make renting floor space at the stadium worthwhile. That was a blow to the club because whilst we did not directly benefit from sales, the shop was important to our image.

There have been other niggly little problems at the ground too. The turnstiles are not big enough for people to pay cash and fans used to just walking up have had to buy tickets. This caused a lot of irritation at first as people found themselves having to queue up twice, first to buy a ticket and then to get in. The system is understood a bit better now but it still seemed ludicrous when games were nowhere near selling out.

The media were hardly given the best first impression of the new ground either as the press box was immediately sealed off as dangerous. Apparently the electricians had installed indoor plug sockets outdoors. It was some while before that was rectified. On top of that, access to the ground has not been great either. The roundabout leading to the entrance was quickly nicknamed kamikaze island by some of us connected to the club because the traffic going up and down the bypass is horrendous and it is difficult to get in and out. People used to criticise Hilton Park for its access but I don't think the new place is any better.

All this sapped my enthusiasm a little. Going down to the club is something I look forward to every day but it got a bit depressing at times in 2009 as all these problems unfolded. Naturally, I find myself pining for the good old days back at Hilton Park. That's a shame because I was really sold on the sports village idea at first. I thought it was going to be a great success and I was very excited during its construction. I thought it would bring Leigh back to life again and I was annoyed that certain people objected when the plans were first drawn up. It made sense in so many ways.

Looking at other clubs, Wigan recognised when the time had come to leave their iconic Central Park ground and Warrington and Hull were revitalised by moves. With the likes of St Helens, Salford, Castleford and Wakefield all wanting new grounds too, we had to move with the times. In addition, it also seemed a great chance to put something into the town, a project that could really regenerate the local economy. Unfortunately the grass is not proving as green as we hoped and I wonder if we really needed to leave Hilton Park. I know it required a lot of work doing to it but over time we could have refurbished the whole place and brought it up to standard. It might not have been state of the art, but even at its worst it was still better than a number of other grounds in Super League. If only we could have built the LSV Stadium at Hilton Park with the club retaining ownership. That would have been perfect.

I know there is no going back now but I don't think I'll ever settle at LSV. I suppose at my age it is difficult to accept change and there has been too much of that with this move. It is not just the new ground that I have really struggled to get used to, but everything that has gone with it. The mentality of the place is so different. It's wonderful that the facilities are used by the wider community but it has been difficult to get my head round the fact we are just one of a number of stadium users.

I'm biased, of course, because Hilton Park was my favourite ground. I thought the old Mather Lane pitch was fantastic, a very good field, but Hilton Park as I remember it has the edge in my affections. After helping build it and then spending so much time there over the 61 years that followed my attachment for it was huge. It held so many memories for me. The games and the people made it so special and I'll never forget how my life changed when I met the man who introduced me to teaching whilst I was working on it. I'll always miss the place and it was sad to see the bulldozers move in. The day they knocked down the Tommy Sale Stand was certainly an emotional one. After that, driving past and seeing open land where the ground once stood was an eerie sight. In time there will be houses there and that to me will seem most strange.

With Hilton Park gone I can now only hope that all these difficulties at LSV prove mere teething troubles because, make no mistake, it is a lovely ground. Press box plugs aside, the contractors did a fine job and it is an arena that befits top-class rugby. It really does give the club great potential. My big fear is the cost of playing there. The club has lurched perilously close to extinction in the past and I don't want to experience that again. Something has to give and I hope common sense prevails because LSV needs Leigh Centurions. The rugby ground is the main feature of the complex and a better arrangement needs to be found.

At the moment we are heavily reliant on Arthur Thomas. He is such a generous man and has put a lot of time and money into the club. I hope he doesn't become disillusioned because if he takes a walk, Leigh rugby league club takes a walk. He's carrying us at the moment and we can't afford to lose him. I don't think people realise what a good job he has done and it annoys me when I hear speccies criticising him. I once told one such disgruntled fan he didn't know what he was talking about but sadly there are a few more like him around. I worry that one day Arthur, with all the other nonsense going on too, might just decide that he has had enough. After all, he is a wealthy man and doesn't need such hassle in his life. We should be grateful we have him.

It is scandalous that people like him should get stick. One man I have the utmost respect for is the Salford chairman John Wilkinson, who is a lovely fella, a real gem. He has put his heart and soul into his club over the course of almost 30 years and backed that up with a lot of investment. Yet still some feel it necessary to criticise him and that sort of attitude makes me sick. He has deserved far more success than he has had and I really hope he fulfils his ambitions for the club.

Yet supporters criticising directors is nothing new. I don't mind it if it is fair comment but all too often people don't find out the facts. Even when things go well the directors can still get it in the neck. I remember some fans questioning what I was doing on the team bus after we won at Wembley in 1971. The fact we always travelled together went over their heads. It can be a thankless task sometimes and that is why I am full of admiration for Arthur and the job he has done.

As we move into 2010, I am hoping Arthur has pulled off another blinder by securing the return of Ian Millward as coach. Arthur, then at Saints, was partly responsible for luring Millward away from us in 2000 and they have retained a good relationship since. Millward is a fine coach who transformed a struggling team last time he was at Leigh. I'm sure he can work that magic again and set the club back on an upward trend, perhaps even to Super League. After our last experience in that competition, I must admit that I'd rather compete at the top of the Championship every year than rejoin the elite and lose every week, but if the finances were right and we could hold our own, it would be very exciting.

The mood of the club has changed with Millward's arrival and I think we'll see a big difference in crowds. Once you lose speccies it is very difficult to get them back but if Millward can rejuvenate the team, as I am sure he will, that will pull people in. There have been some good new signings, such as Robbie Paul and Ricky Bibey, and on paper we should be a lot stronger. I have always believed the essence of a good side is pace and power; the two Ps. You need pace in the backs and power in the forwards. Hopefully we'll be strong in both areas and the enthusiasm of the fans picks up. Leigh is a rugby town and if the team is winning, people will come.

I didn't think last year's squad looked too bad but it didn't gel and discipline was poor. We had some good players but they didn't play together and they conceded too many costly penalties. At the end of the day there could be no complaints about where we finished, but that is in the past now. We have been given another chance and must make the most of it. It will be a tough year with games against good teams such as Widnes and Halifax but, as ever at the start of a season, I am confident.

I'm also hugely encouraged by our youth set-up. Our Academy side won their league in 2009 and that is a very good sign. The town has always produced good players and it is great to see that continuing. I just hope we are able to keep hold of them. That has not always been the case in the past. Nearly all the teams we play against have Leigh lads in their side and I often wonder how strong we would be if we had not lost them. Unfortunately we have not been able to compete with the wages on offer elsewhere, but that is something we will have to live with for now. We have learnt the hard way how foolhardy it is to overspend and we cannot put the club's future wellbeing at risk. It would be nice to be rubbing shoulders with Leeds and St Helens again but we have to build steadily and not overstretch ourselves. Those clubs are miles ahead of us and the contracts they can offer players are astounding. To get back into Super League we have to ensure that absolutely everything is in place and we are ready to compete. There are no short cuts.

As I have explained elsewhere, though, I don't like the licensing system. I can understand the reasoning behind it and it may be good for the clubs already in Super League, but it detracts from the other competitions. There is much less incentive for players at Championship level when there is no automatic promotion to aim for. I miss the excitement of the old two-up, two-down format.

Millward takes over as coach in 2010 from one of Leigh's greatest servants of recent times, Paul Rowley, who reverts to the role of assistant that he held under previous coach-turned-director of rugby Neil Kelly. I hope Paul learns from him and goes on to be a successful coach in his own right one day. I have always admired him, right from his younger days as a hooker. He inherited a lot of the enthusiasm of his father, our chief executive and former player Allan Rowley, and never shied away from anything. He was a superb player who was in England's World Cup squad in 2000 and it was unfortunate he left us for spells at Halifax and Huddersfield. He really is Leigh through and through and is a great asset to the club.

I have seen many fine players over the years and it has been both a pleasure and privilege to have been involved with this great sport for so long. Little could I have imagined at 10 how much a request to help operate a scoreboard would define my life. From that moment on rugby league became my passion and, despite all the trials and tribulations of the decades since, my enthusiasm for it has rarely dipped. The game owes me nothing, but I owe it a lot. It has given me a wonderful life and I cannot imagine how things would have been without it. Even now, people are always stopping me to talk about rugby league and I love it. I just hope that one day, perhaps, I might finally be allowed to forget dropping that ball!

My All-Time Favourites

As is traditional, I'd like to conclude by selecting my all-time favourite XIIIs. I may never have taken to coaching in real life but in the world of fantasy there are a lot of great players I would have loved to have sent out on the same field together. I'll start with my greatest ever Leigh team and then look at my all-time favourites.

GREATEST LEIGH XIII

1: Jimmy Ledgard

(334 Leigh appearances between 1948-58)

There was no competition for the full-back berth. Jimmy was a fantastic player, as I have detailed elsewhere. He could catch anything you threw at him and his kicking ability was a joy to behold.

2: Des Drummond

(278; 1976-86)

One of the fastest wingers that has ever played the game. Not very big, but very strong and very effective. A top finisher and a robust tackler.

3: Trevor Allan

(97; 1951-53)

A great Australian import. He arrived after I left but what I saw of him was impressive, particularly his defence. He was just awesome in that discipline. He used to tackle players from behind with incredible ferocity.

4: Teddy Kerwick

(202; 1947-53)

Teddy was a bit of a loner off the field, a very quiet lad, but on it he was an outstanding performer. A very strong runner who always fed his winger at the right time.

5: Bill Kindon

(259; 1949-59)

Wingers need pace and Bill had it in abundance. He was a centre's dream and I would have loved to have played alongside him more than I did. He smoked like a chimney but still had incredible energy.

6: John Woods

(343; 1976-92)

The complete player. John Woods was born to play rugby. He had a great sidestep and turn of pace, could score tries and kick goals. He could also tackle, although it was remarkable he never dislocated his shoulder with his one-arm technique. I wonder how great he could have been had he been more committed.

7: Alex Murphy

(113; 1967-71)

Alex Murphy OBE was the greatest player and motivator the club has ever had. I mention the OBE because he'll get upset if I don't! Murphy transformed the Leigh team and memories of his success live on. He not only led by example but knew how to get the best out of players. A true legend.

8: Stan Owen

(415; 1951-64)

A real tough nut, Stan could give as good as he got but he also had a bit more to his game. If opponents wanted it rough, they got it rough, but if they preferred it smooth, Stan showed he had a bit of class too.

9: Kevin Ashcroft

(256; 1967-77)

A very good hooker in the days when hookers were hookers. Anyone can play there these days – at a lot of scrums the ball is virtually put in at the loose forward's feet – but back then you needed a good one to get it. Kevin was rarely beaten.

10: Bill Robinson

(391; 1953-67)

Not quite as rough as Stan but fairly tough and someone who always gave 100%. The pack was immeasurably stronger with him in it.

11: Charlie Pawsey

(216; 1947-55)

An extremely tough and very aggressive forward. He took some stopping and when he tackled you, you knew about it.

12: Mick Martyn

(328; 1954-67)

Mick was ahead of his time, a great tryscoring second row in the days when they were a rarity. He had terrific speed off the mark and was one of the outstanding players of his era. A great servant to the club.

13: Peter Foster

(236; 1951-58)

An extremely good defensive loose forward. If Peter put his hand on a player he was down, it was as simple as that. He was a great tackler. Sadly lost to the club when he was tragically killed in a car crash.

ALL-TIME GREATEST XIII

1: Jim Sullivan

(Wigan)

Like Ledgard, Jim was an incredible kicker. He could place it anywhere he wanted and his goalkicking was deadly accurate from any angle. His catching of the ball was also immaculate. He just never dropped them.

2: Brian Bevan

(Warrington)

Appearances were certainly deceptive. Brian did not look like a rugby player but he was a natural blessed with incredible speed. He was so fast and used to swerve past opponents as if they were not there.

3: Ernest Ward

(Bradford)

A terrific centre with a good pair of hands, a great turn of speed and strong defence. One of my great contemporaries.

4: Keith Senior

(Leeds)

This choice might raise eyebrows but what I have seen of Senior over the past decade puts him up there with the best. He is a strong runner, very dangerous near the line and is difficult to tackle. I once saw him score two tries in one game from his own 20, outpacing everyone. It was superb. He is also good defensively and would have excelled in any era.

5: Tom Van Vollenhoven

(St Helens)

Another magnificent winger. The South African had great pace and was doubly difficult to tackle because of his strength. He scored tries by the bucketload.

6: Willie Horne

(Barrow)

A tricky player who was always capable of making a break or creating an opening for a support runner. A fine goalkicker too.

7: Alex Murphy

(St Helens/Leigh)

Murphy's success at Leigh owed much to his motivational qualities but on pure playing, he was one of the greatest scrum-halves ever to lace boots. He was like lightning off the mark, particularly on the blindside. His aggression and cheek – there was no-one cheekier – made him formidable.

8: Ken Gee

(Wigan)

A big, robust prop who could hold his own with anybody in the pack. A real powerhouse at Wigan for many years and an established international.

9: Joe Egan

(Wigan)

One of the great hookers of his day and his partnership with Gee was awesome. Another long-serving Wiganer and a fine international player.

10: Frank Whitcombe

(Bradford)

Another very big forward who took some stopping once he got running. A player who helped make Bradford such a feared proposition in the 1940s.

11: Charlie Pawsey

(Leigh)

As an England and Great Britain international in the early 1950s, Charlie would have held his own in any pack.

12: Trevor Foster

(Bradford)

The amount of work Trevor got through in a game was incredible. He never gave less than 100% and if I had to pick a captain for this team, it would be him.

13: Ken Traill

(Bradford)

Very few scrum-halves got the better of Ken. Anyone that went round the blindside did so at their own risk when he was around. A real livewire loose forward.

Tributes to Tommy Sale

COLIN HUTTON

Former Widnes team-mate, now president of Hull KR

I remember vividly when Tommy arrived at Widnes. He came from out of town, which was unusual in those days, but he was like a breath of fresh air. He soon became captain and if ever there was a description of an inspirational skipper, it was him. We regarded him as a kind of elder statesman. He was a very good player too, definitely county standard, and we looked up to him very much.

He was a great character and we came to know him as 'Gluke' because he used to bring these glucose drinks with him before each match. He swore by them and we used to take it religiously. I'm sure he did mix sherry in. Remarkably, he was captaining an amateur team before Widnes picked him up. He had apparently all but retired so to go from there to captaining a team at Wembley in the space of a season was a great story, perhaps unique.

The best game we played together, when he played left centre and I played right, was undoubtedly against Bradford Northern in the 1950 Challenge Cup semi-final at Wigan. We scored the points between us in a famous victory. He claimed two tries and I kicked a goal. It was a wonderful achievement for us because Bradford were a brilliant team, having played in the three previous Wembley finals. The two centres opposite us that day were the Great Britain pairing of Jack Kitching and Ernest Ward and getting the better of them is something that always stands out in my mind.

I can't speak highly enough of Tommy's efforts. I really enjoyed playing with him and loved his company. We became firm friends and socialised quite a lot together with our wives. He took us for many a good night out in Leigh. Unfortunately we were only team-mates for a year because I left Widnes for Hull in 1951 but our friendship endures to this day. I don't see too much of him nowadays but whenever a Leigh team comes to Hull Kingston Rovers, Tommy is always part of the entourage. It's always great to catch up.

I'll always remember the inspiration Tommy brought to the Widnes dressing room and I've nothing but lovely memories of him.

ALEX MURPHY

Leigh player/coach 1966-1971, coach 1980-1982, 1985, 1990-91

I have always liked Tommy. He is a 100% genuine man and I would trust him with my life. I have never heard anybody say a bad word about him and I am sure that is true throughout rugby league.

He played a big role in my career story as the man chiefly responsible for taking me to Leigh. It was seen as quite an audacious move at the time but he was determined to get his man and that was typical of him. His heart and soul was in trying to do the best for Leigh. He had probably been sitting in his car for about three hours waiting for me to come off the golf course when he first approached me – and I told him where to go. It wasn't just that he was asking me to go to Leigh, but what he was asking me to do. I was only 27 and playing for St Helens – the biggest club in rugby league – and he wanted me to coach at Leigh, having never coached in my life.

It seemed preposterous but he obviously understood how my mind ticked and persuaded me to think about it. I didn't know I could coach, but Tommy obviously did. The seed he planted in my head grew and I'm glad that he stuck to his guns because we went on to have a great time at Leigh and do exceptionally well.

Tommy and I became really good friends whilst I was at Leigh. We helped each other a lot as I fed off his confidence and he mine. He was great to work with and everything we said we'd do we went out and did. We had a lot of very happy moments together.

Tommy's selfless devotion to the Leigh cause is astounding. I certainly cannot think of one bad thing he has ever done for the club. He has given them his life and done more for them than probably anybody else. He has been totally dedicated both on and off the field and if they are putting up statues they should put up one of him. But, above all, he is simply a number one great man. He loves rugby and loves people and is not far off being the perfect fella.

MICK MARTYN

Leigh 1954-1967

I'm surprised and disappointed Tommy has never been included on any Honours List. It's a shame to see other people far less deserving awarded honours. It's very rare you find someone like Tommy prepared to give 60 years' service to one club – and that's just since he finished playing. For me there is no more deserving person and a lot of other people have said it too.

People call Tommy 'Mr Leigh', and that's very fitting because it's his life. I have known him for many years at the club and he is very highly respected. I get on with him very well, as everyone does. He is a true gentleman and is very quiet and unassuming. When I was playing he was always very supportive and we spoke a lot. He made you feel good. They recently named the new road Sale Way after him and that is a nice and deserved honour. Nobody has a bad word to say about him.

DAVE CHISNALL

Leigh 1967-1971, 1976-1977

Mr Sale, as we used to call him, was a gentleman. He was the man who first saw me playing amateur rugby as an 18-year-old and asked me if I wanted to sign for Leigh. At first I was shocked and unsure what to do. They were offering me £250 but I wanted to speak to my mother and brothers about it first. They thought I was better than that and should hold out for more but after next meeting Mr Sale I just knew Leigh was the right club. I got a great feeling for the place and knew I was going to be settled there.

Tommy was also instrumental in bringing Alex Murphy to Leigh. He gave Alex a great opportunity to coach and play at Leigh and it paid handsome dividends. It was a great era to be part of. I realise it mustn't have been nice when Alex came back and took some players, myself included, after leaving for Warrington but I'm sure he still thinks tremendously of Tommy. Personally, I'll never forget Tommy and what he did for me.

Tommy was always good company too. He frequently mixed with the players, although I can't remember any funny escapades involving him. I think that's the kind of person he was – tunnel vision Leigh and tunnel vision players. If ever you mentioned a player might be worth looking at he'd make sure he checked him out. He was forever watching amateur games.

And he is still as devoted as ever. He's a tremendous

figurehead, he's Mr Leigh. When I hear people talk about everything he's done I wonder just what he hasn't done. He's done everything for Leigh and is still doing an incredible job. He'll never tire of it. He's a fantastic man.

JOHN WOODS

Leigh 1976-1985, 1990-1992

I've known Tommy for 40-odd years. When I played junior rugby for Butts CE we'd often come up against his St Peter's team and I also got to know him through the Leigh town side. As a Leigh supporter I knew plenty about him too and when I eventually signed for the club I found him a great person to have around. He was very much a man of the players. He always wanted to speak to everybody and make himself known. We liked him so much because he was not only a rugby man but a true gentleman and great to talk to.

He's been a stalwart for Leigh for many years in many roles. To think he was involved in rugby before the War and is still going strong now is remarkable and the amount of voluntary work he must have done over the years is incredible. He's one great bloke and all the praise he gets is fully justified. They named Sale Way after him and he thoroughly deserves such an honour.

KEITH LATHAM

Leigh Centurions head coach 1996-1998,
now chairman of Leigh East ARLFC

I've known Tommy for more than 40 years and he's been an inspiration to me and to everyone in rugby in Leigh as a whole. Tommy understands the game of rugby league possibly better than anyone else on this planet. He's been here 91 years and I reckon he's probably been involved in rugby for 99% of them. He cares so much about the game and the people involved in it and that always shines through. On top of that, he's a nice man to boot.

When I was head coach at Leigh the support given to me by Tommy was very comforting, but it is his contribution to rugby and the town as a whole that I'd like to draw attention to. As well as everything he does for the Centurions, he's still very much a grassroots person of the game. I want to thank him for his work with the children of Leigh and in the amateur game. He has always been willing to help out and is a regular and welcome visitor at Leigh East, where he is rightly revered. He opened our new clubhouse on Boxing Day 2008 and when we set up a girls team recently, it was Tommy who paid for their kit. It was a wonderful and selfless gesture in keeping with the man.

When I was involved with the Academy team at Leigh Tommy never used to miss a game, home or away, rain or shine. I can still see him now, sat with us on the bench at Bradford with a blanket wrapped around his legs, cheering the lads on. He always wanted to be in the thick of it and still does. He's been involved in the game at every level, from junior to professional, on and off the field. His commitment and dedication to the game and Leigh has been magnificent and you don't see that very often.

My face beams whenever I see Tommy walk into a room. He's a very special person with a wicked sense of humour that I love. I could sit and listen to him for hours. I really can't give him enough plaudits.

PAUL ROWLEY

Leigh assistant coach, Leigh player 1993-1994, 2002-2007

Some people say I must be Tommy Sale's apprentice because of the way I have come through the ranks at Leigh but I'll have to go some to match his commitment. He has been part of the furniture at the club for so long and his passion for the club has never wavered as long as I have known him. On the first away trip of every season I can guarantee he will sit next to me at the front of the bus with his wine gums and ask me to name everyone he doesn't know. He likes to know who is who and keep up to speed with everything that is going on.

He is the most familiar face at the club and comes in to see us every day, always smartly dressed. All we want to do now is win some silverware to put a smile on his face, because he deserves it.

We have occasionally given Tommy a bit of trouble. One successful year the lads started to get a bit giddy after games, as youngsters do, and Tommy, who was prone to falling asleep on the bus, had a couple of his trilbies pinched. One of them came with us all round Manchester on a 'Mad Monday' and I think all of us took a turn to wear it at some point before it got lost. We bought him a new one as soon as we could and thankfully I don't think he was too disheartened.

Tommy is a great character who is popular with everyone. He's been there and done it all and has probably achieved more in his lifetime than most people ever will. He is very highly respected by all at Leigh, young and old.

IAN MILLWARD

Leigh Centurions head coach 1998-2000, 2009-present

When I came to Leigh back in 1998, the first person I met was Tommy. He worked in the office at Hilton Park. My first impression was that here was an older guy who would have the Leigh club at heart but would be very traditionalist. But I found after only a short period that I just used to love sitting down to talk to him about rugby league. He just had a really open view of the game and his lateral thinking on it was really good, as was his perception of the modern game. His sharpness on rugby league was outstanding and he was a guy I respected very much.

Tommy is one of the men who have set a lot of the morals we have in rugby league. He is very well respected by everyone, not just in Leigh but elsewhere. When I came back to Leigh last year, on my first day I picked him up and went for lunch with him and the chairman. He hadn't changed at all. He was still sharp with some really good thoughts, very loyal, always talking rugby league. He's got a great sense of humour and zest for life. If Leigh are successful he'll be at the forefront of it. He is part and parcel of everything at Leigh. He's become really good friends with my mum and dad too. They're always asking how he is. He's just a really nice person.

ARTHUR THOMAS

Leigh Centurions chairman

Tommy has the respect of everyone. Wherever you go, people want to wish him well. Every few weeks we go out for lunch and people always recognise him. On one occasion a waitress addressed him as Mr Sale. I asked her how she knew him and it was because he taught her mother. How many people respect their parents' teachers like that?

Another time we went to a Widnes-St Helens match together. When the Widnes past players saw him, they didn't ask, "How are you Tommy?" but "How are you Mr Sale?" That's the kind of respect people have for him and it's the same throughout rugby league. Wherever you are, nobody has a bad word for him.

ALLAN ROWLEY

Leigh Centurions chief executive, Leigh player 1971-1979

Tommy Sale's name is synonymous with rugby league in Leigh and it is a name I have been associated with all my life. I've known Tommy for almost 50 years having been coached by him when I played in the Leigh schoolboys side. He is a great ambassador, not only for the club but the town in general.

Tommy has done everything for the club from playing to being secretary to be being director. His commitment has been remarkable. I remember the days when players used to be paid in cash and Tommy would go to the bank every week and count it out into envelopes. He was so thorough that if there was 2p left over at the end he would undo them all and start again. That was an absolute nightmare for us at times but his dedication was beyond question. His heart is still 100% in the club today.

It is probably a slight exaggeration to say he saved my life that day when I collapsed and I don't remember these stories about me 'sticking one' on opponents quite like Tommy does, but I consider myself very privileged to have known him. I had the honour of compering his 90th birthday party at Leigh Miners and that was quite a night. Tommy had been expecting a few old friends and family and was staggered when about 250 people turned up. That shows the esteem with which he is held and I think he's wonderful.

LORD PETER SMITH

Leader of Wigan Council and Leigh supporter

I am too young to remember Tommy Sale as a player but my first memories of him are of his sweet shop by the bus station and Regal Cinema where I spent some of my pocket money. When I asked who this Tommy Sale was, I was told he was a famous rugby player and occasionally he would serve in the shop, which was a great treat for us kids.

Later I became aware of Tommy's huge contribution to Leigh Rugby League Football Club. In both good and less good times he has been a true servant of the club doing many unrecognised backroom tasks as well as performing his more public role as timekeeper. When the council came to recognise contributions to the local community in choosing 10 new Freemen of the Borough to celebrate the Millennium, Tommy was an obvious choice.

At an event to celebrate Billy Boston's 50 years in the borough, Tommy was called on stage with Colin Tyrer, Frankie Parr and Georgie Fame and the audience was asked for the connection. The answer was they had all played rugby under Tommy.

As we began to plan Leigh Sports Village, Tommy used to say to me, "It is a great project for Leigh but will it be built in my lifetime?" I am delighted that it has been completed so that Tommy can experience much better conditions in his continuing work for Leigh.

PLAYERS
AND
OFFICIALS
ONLY

Tommy Sale's Career Stats

Season	*Club*	*A*	*T*	*G*	*PTS*
1938-39	Leigh	9	1	2	7
1939-40	Leigh	2	2	0	6
1940-41	Leigh	1	0	0	0
1946-47	Leigh	33	6	0	18
1947-48	Leigh	26	6	0	18
1948-49	Leigh	11	1	0	3
	LEIGH TOTAL	**82**	**16**	**2**	**52**
1945-46	Warrington (*guest*)	7	1	0	3
1949-50	Widnes	25	12	0	36
1950-51	Widnes	9	1	1	5
	WIDNES TOTAL	**34**	**13**	**1**	**41**

If you enjoyed this, you'll love these from Scratching Shed Publishing Ltd...

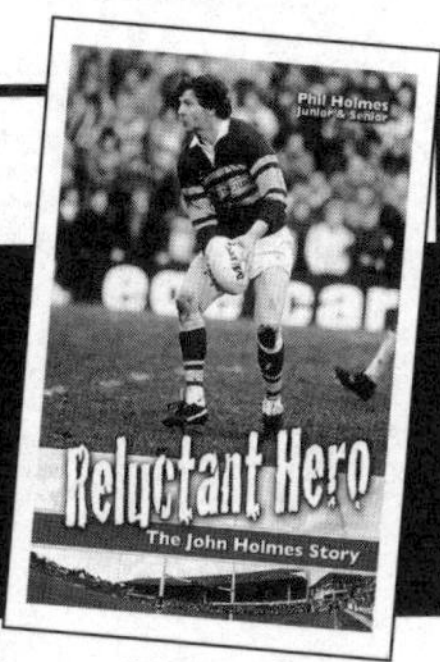

Reluctant Hero

The John Holmes Story

The OFFICIAL and FAMILY-APPROVED biography of the late Leeds and Great Britain rugby league legend John Holmes. Uniquely told by his brother and nephew, it is littered with anecdotes and reminiscences from friends and former team mates. The definitive life of one of the code's greats.

PUBLISHED APRIL 2010 - ISBN: 978-0956252647

From Hull to Hell and Back

The autobiography of Lee Crooks

After bursting on the scene as a gifted teenager, rugby league prop Lee Crooks was an archetypal blood and guts heart-on-his-sleeve firebrand front-rower, whether with his hometown Hull, Leeds, Castleford or Great Britain. Told for the first time, this is the always colourful and often controversial story of a modern-day rugby league colossus - on and off the field!

ON SALE 30 JUNE 2010 ISBN: **978-0956252685**

Off The Ropes

The Ron Lyle Story - by Candace Toft

In a life as tough and brutal as his bouts, Ron Lyle had already served time for second degree murder before he began his boxing career. Later, he was the supposedly third-rate fighter who had Muhammad Ali beat for ten rounds; the guy who knocked George Foreman down four times; and the guy who was arrested for murder a second time.

ON SALE 14 MAY 2010 ISBN: **978-0956252623**

Scratching Shed Publishing Ltd

Scratching Shed Publishing Ltd is an independent publishing company founded in May 2008. We aim to produce high-quality books covering a wide range of subjects - including sport, travel and popular culture - of worldwide interest yet with the distinctive flavour of the North of England.

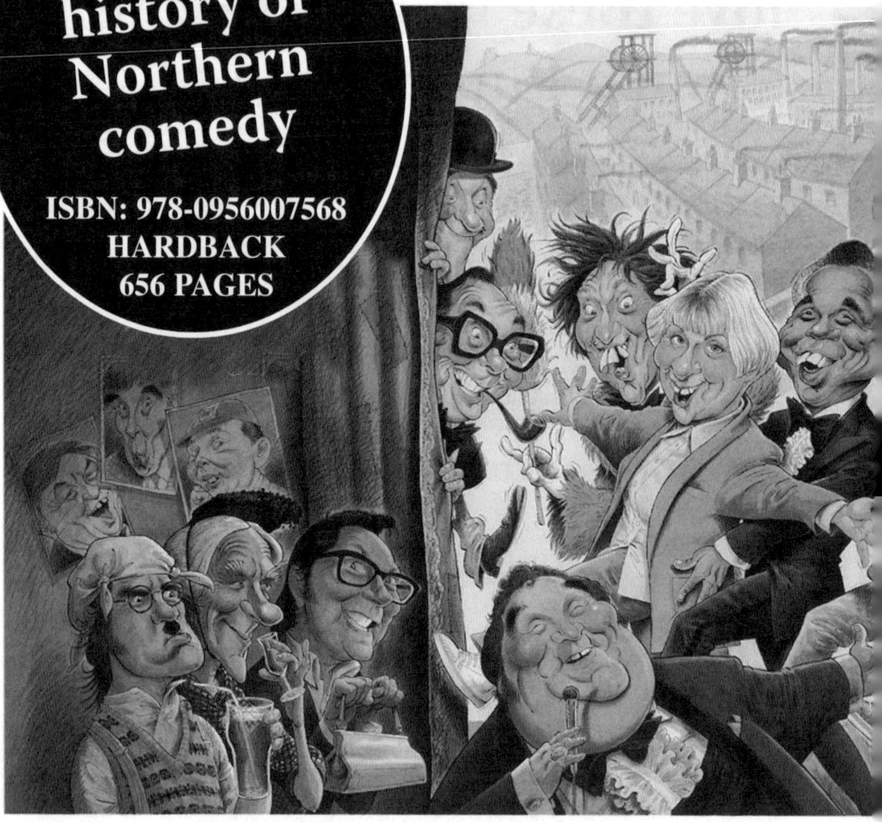

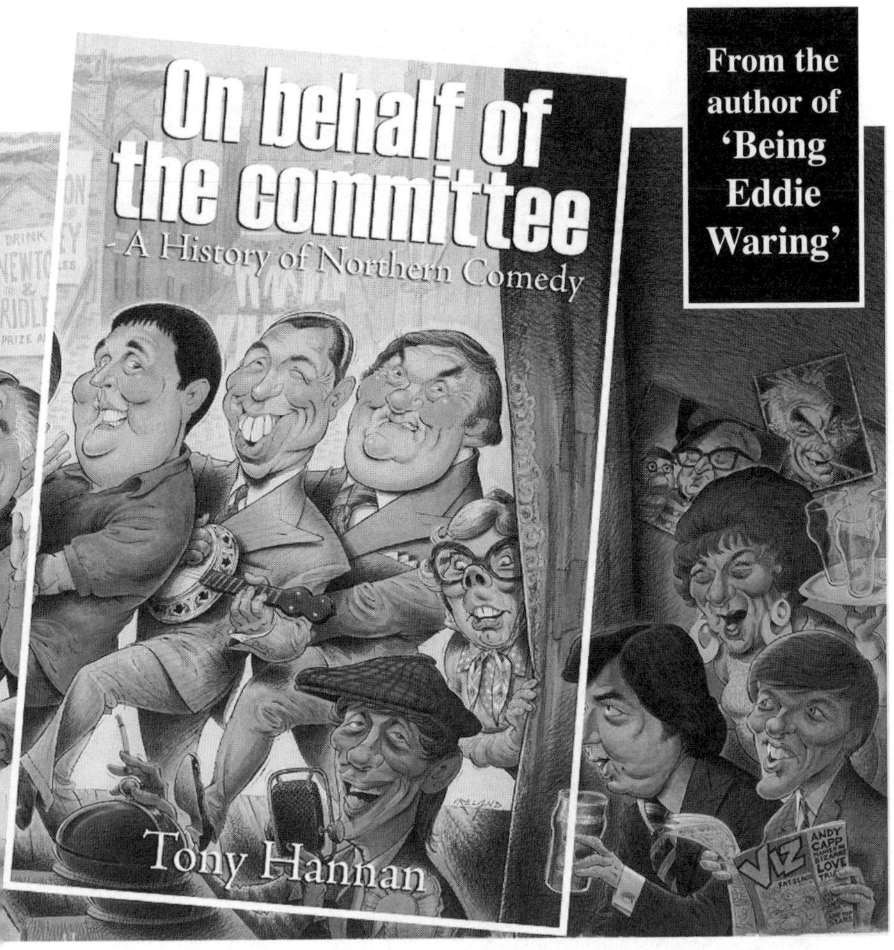

From the Industrial Revolution to our own comfortable 21st century digital age - via music hall, Variety, working mens clubs, radio, cinema & television - Northern-born comedians have consistently been at the heart of popular British comedy culture, tickling the funny bone of the entire nation.

This witty and informative book questions why that should be so, all the while charting an entertaining course through the careers of George Formby, Tommy Handley, Gracie Fields, Frank Randle, Al Read, Jimmy James, Hylda Baker, Jimmy Clitheroe, Les Dawson, Morecambe & Wise, Bernard Manning, Alan Bennett, Monty Python, Victoria Wood, Ken Dodd, Chubby Brown, The Young Ones, Vic and Bob, Steve Coogan, Caroline Aherne, the League of Gentlemen, Johnny Vegas, Peter Kay and many many others. Along the way, it also wonders why such a huge contribution to the British entertainment industry should be so often under-appreciated.

Mostly, however, it is a rich celebration of British comedy history & confirmation that you really do have to laugh - or else you'd cry...

Also out now or coming soon from Scratching Shed Publishing Ltd...

In The Prison Of His Days

The Memoirs of a Captured World War II Gunner

When Gunner Norman Davison returned to Sheffield after the Second World War, he wrote down a vivid account of his experiences. Here, published for the very first time, is the result: a singular tale of extraordinary times, that is by turns moving, amusing, informative and thrilling.

OUT NOW - ISBN: 9780956007582

Out of the Blue

A Policeman's Story of Life and Death - by David Watson

A lifetime of policing the streets - but that was only the beginning. For years, PC David Watson was a copper of the old school. He patrolled the towns and cities of England's north by car and on foot, where a fight against crime lurked around every corner. Until one day disaster struck, albeit from an unlikely source leaving him with a gruelling and gruesome fight for life.

ON SALE 31 JULY 2010 ISBN: **978-0956252630**

Last of the Dinosaurs

The Kevin Ashcroft Story - by Maurice Bamford

Last of the Dinosaurs charts the eventful, brutal & often controversial career of Kevin Ashcroft - a man thought by many to be the first truly modern rugby league hooker. Awash with incident and anecdote, this is an entertaining read, detailing Ashcroft's stints with Warrington, Leigh, Salford, Dewsbury & Rochdale among much else.

OUT NOW ISBN: 9780956007520

Scratching Shed Publishing Ltd

Scratching Shed Publishing Ltd is an independent publishing company founded in May 2008. We aim to produce high-quality books covering a wide range of subjects - including sport, travel and popular culture - of worldwide interest yet with the distinctive flavour of the North of England.

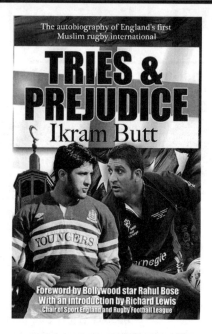

Past deeds. Present voices.

Introducing Rugby League Classics - an ongoing series of historically significant rugby league books - rediscovered, rebranded and republished in paperback, often after having been long out-of-print.

Each edition comes complete with the original manuscript intact, and contains a wealth of new and updated material, including an introductory overview written by a relevant modern-day expert, evocative photographs, appendices, an index and the modern-day recollections of those closest to the book's primary subject, i.e. family members, former team-mates and other contemporary figures.

It is anticipated that at least two such titles will published every year, covering a wide range of eras and celebrated rugby league personalities.

To stay right up to date with news of all our latest releases, simply drop an email to **news@scratchingshedpublishing.com** and we will add you to our mailing list.

Rugby League Classics

OUT NOW - Numbers 1-4

- Gus Risman
- Lewis Jones
- Eric Ashton
- XIII Winters, XIII Worlds

Visit our website:

www.scratchingshedpublishing.co.uk

Scratching Shed Publishing Ltd

Treasure the old. Embrace the new.